COSSACK FAIRY TALES

AND

FOLK-TALES.

ILLUSTRATED BY E. W. MITCHELL.

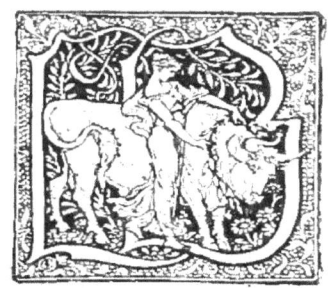

Cossack

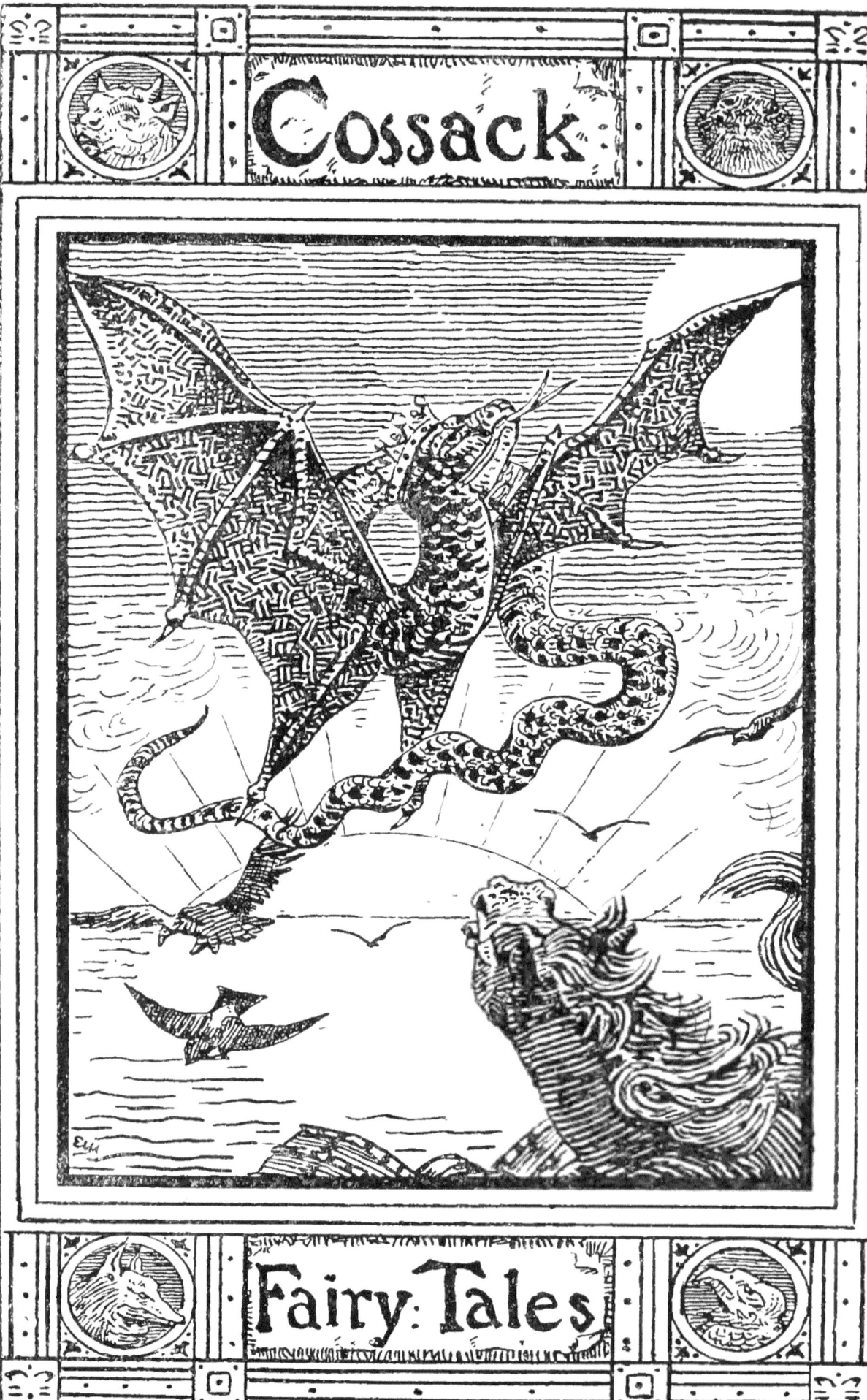

Fairy Tales

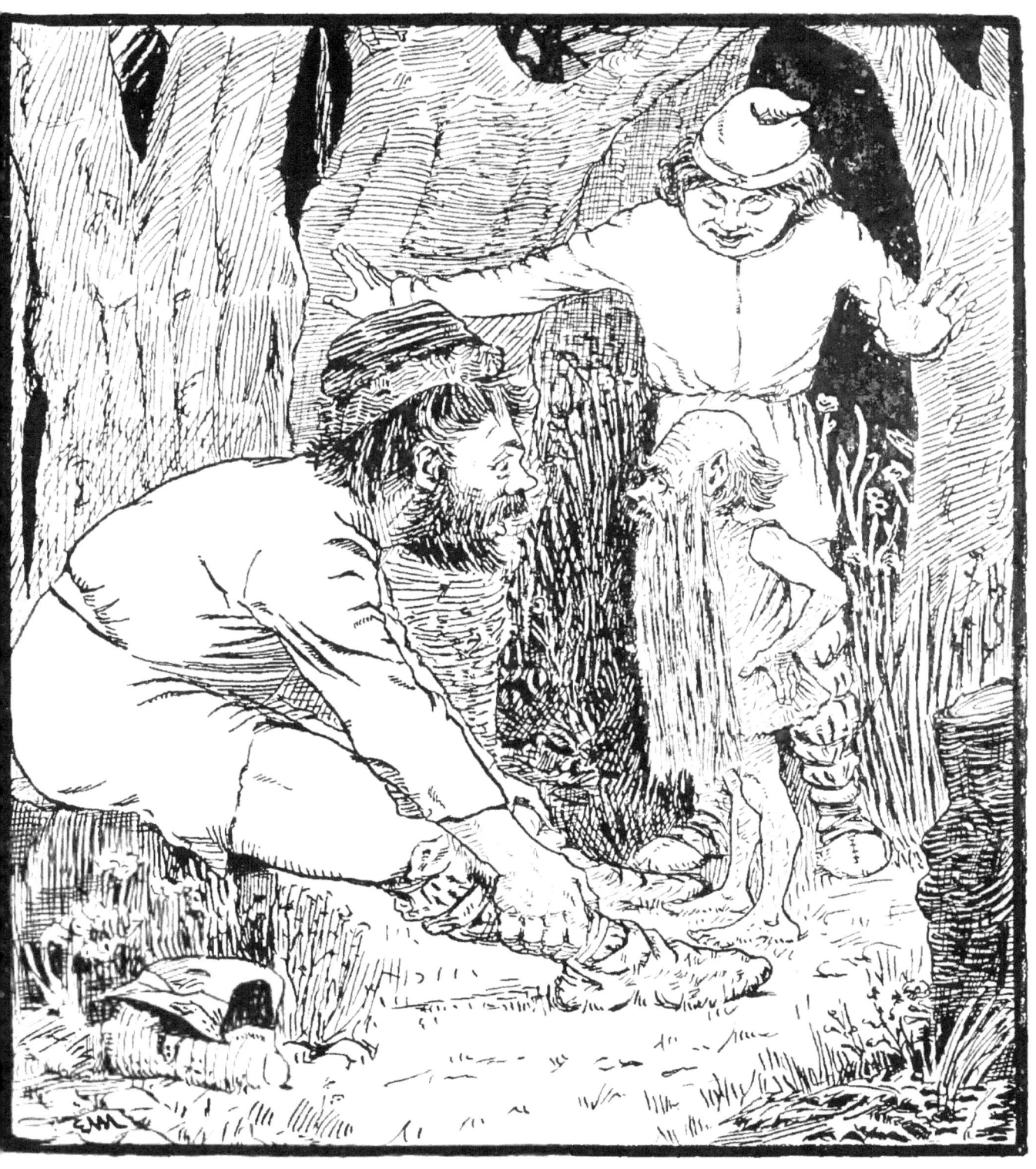

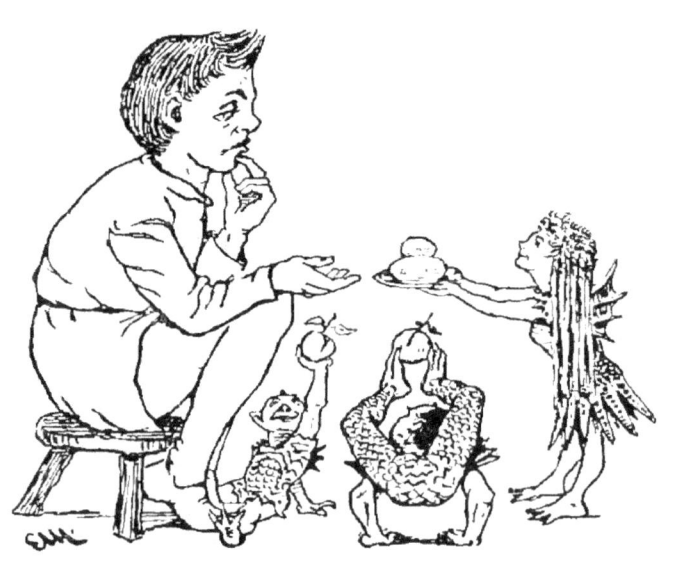

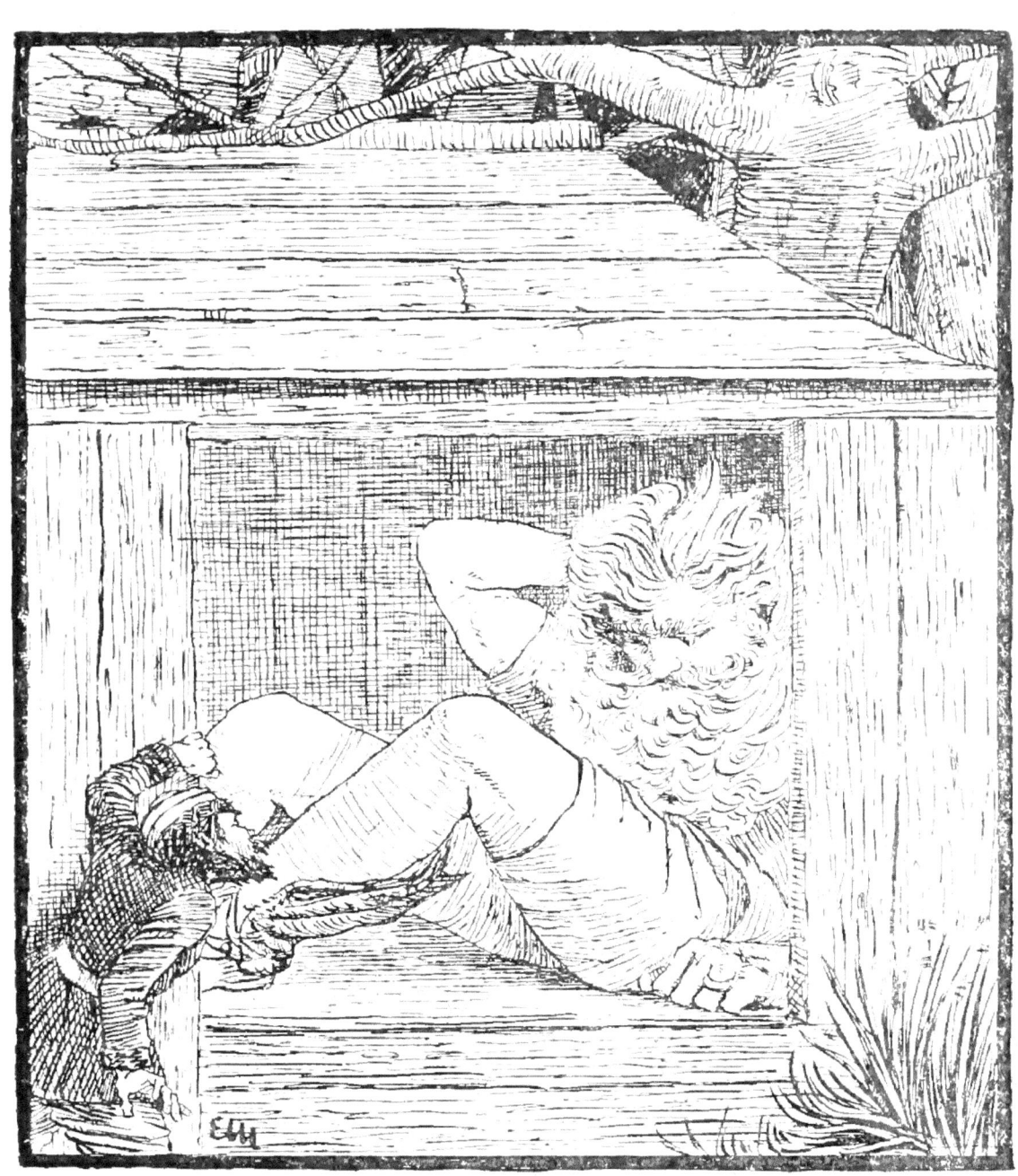

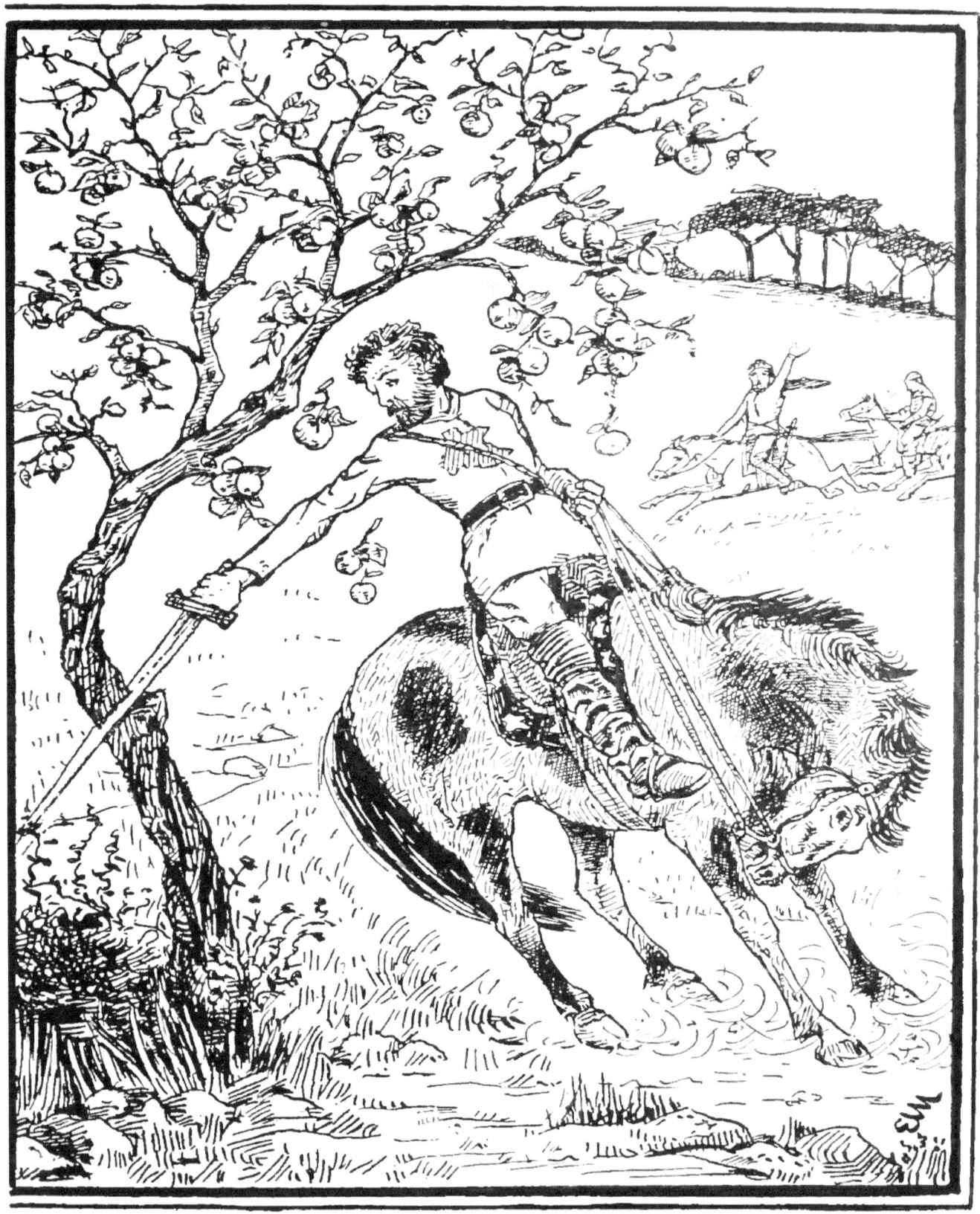

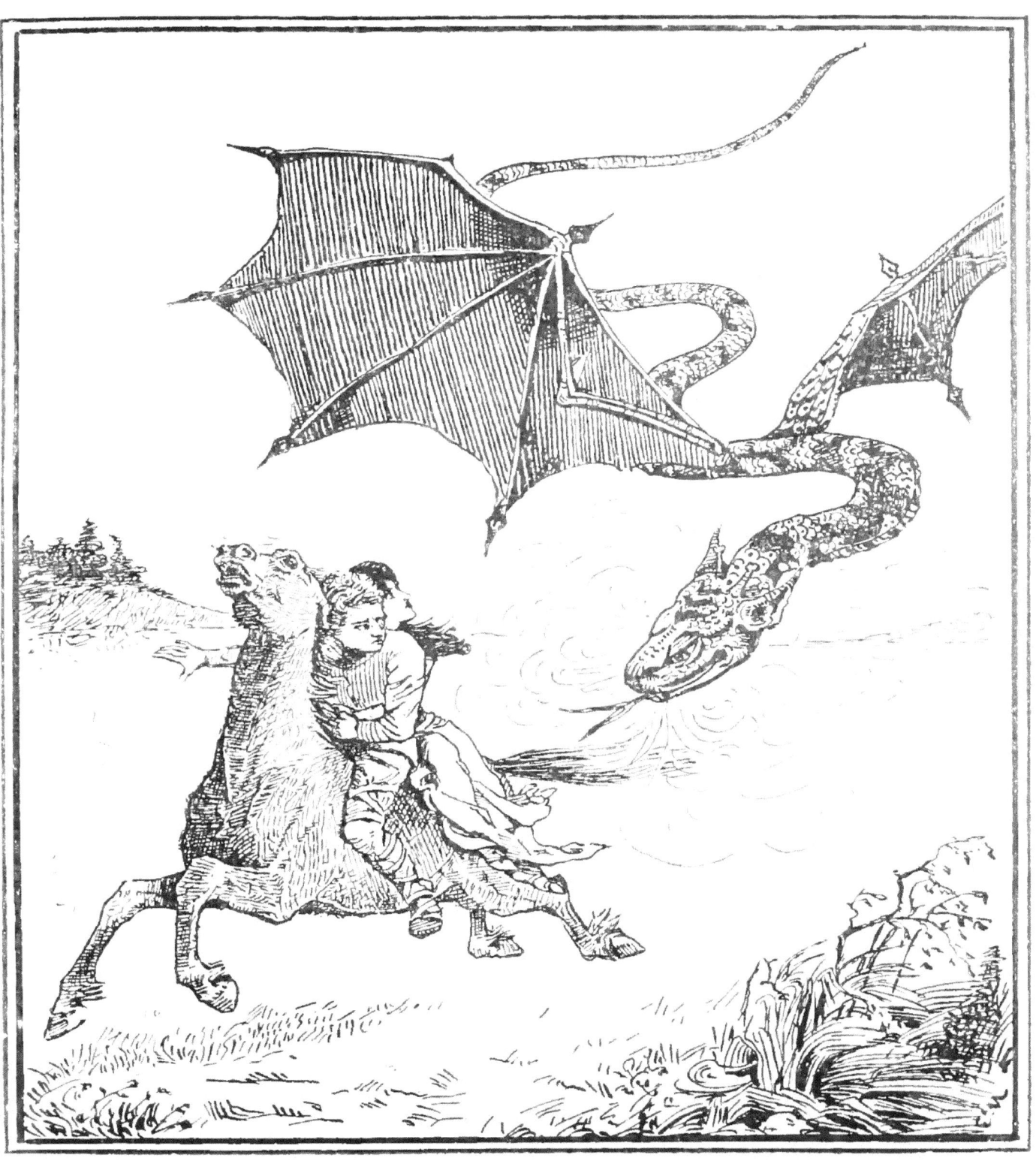

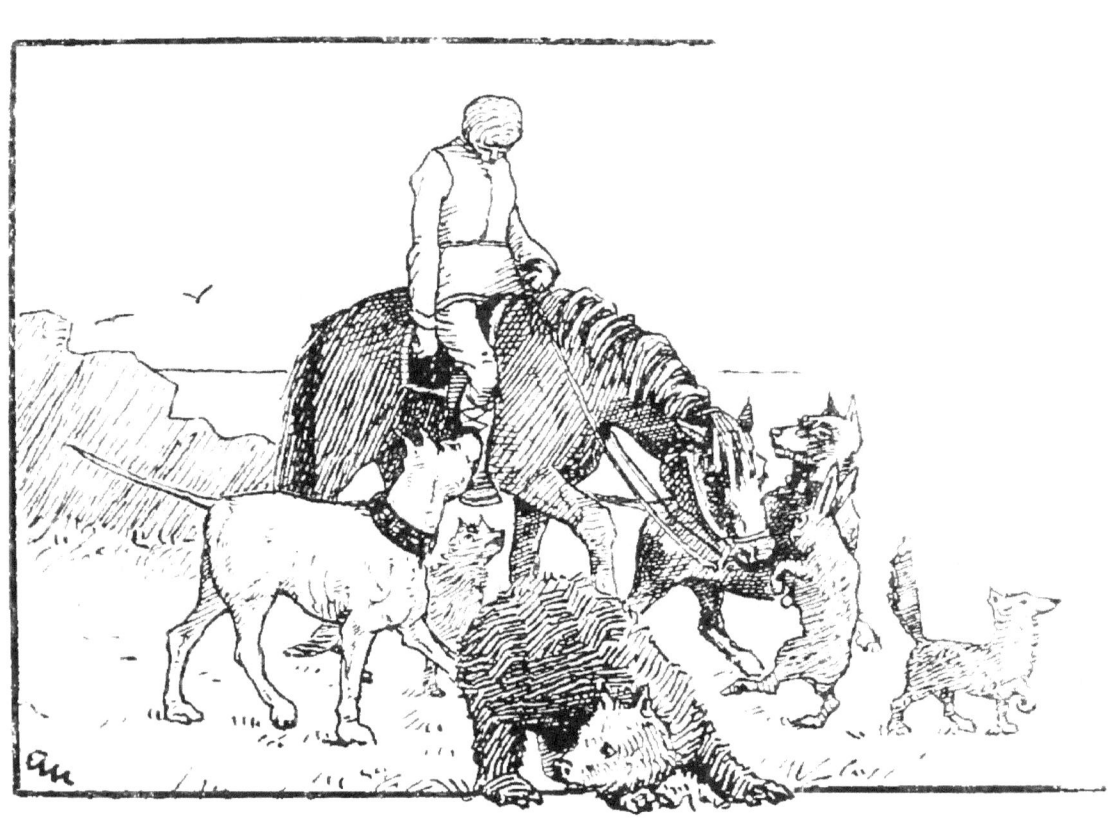

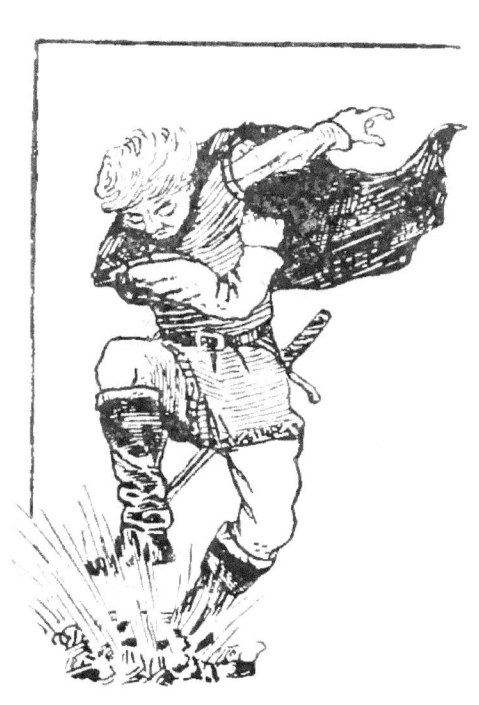

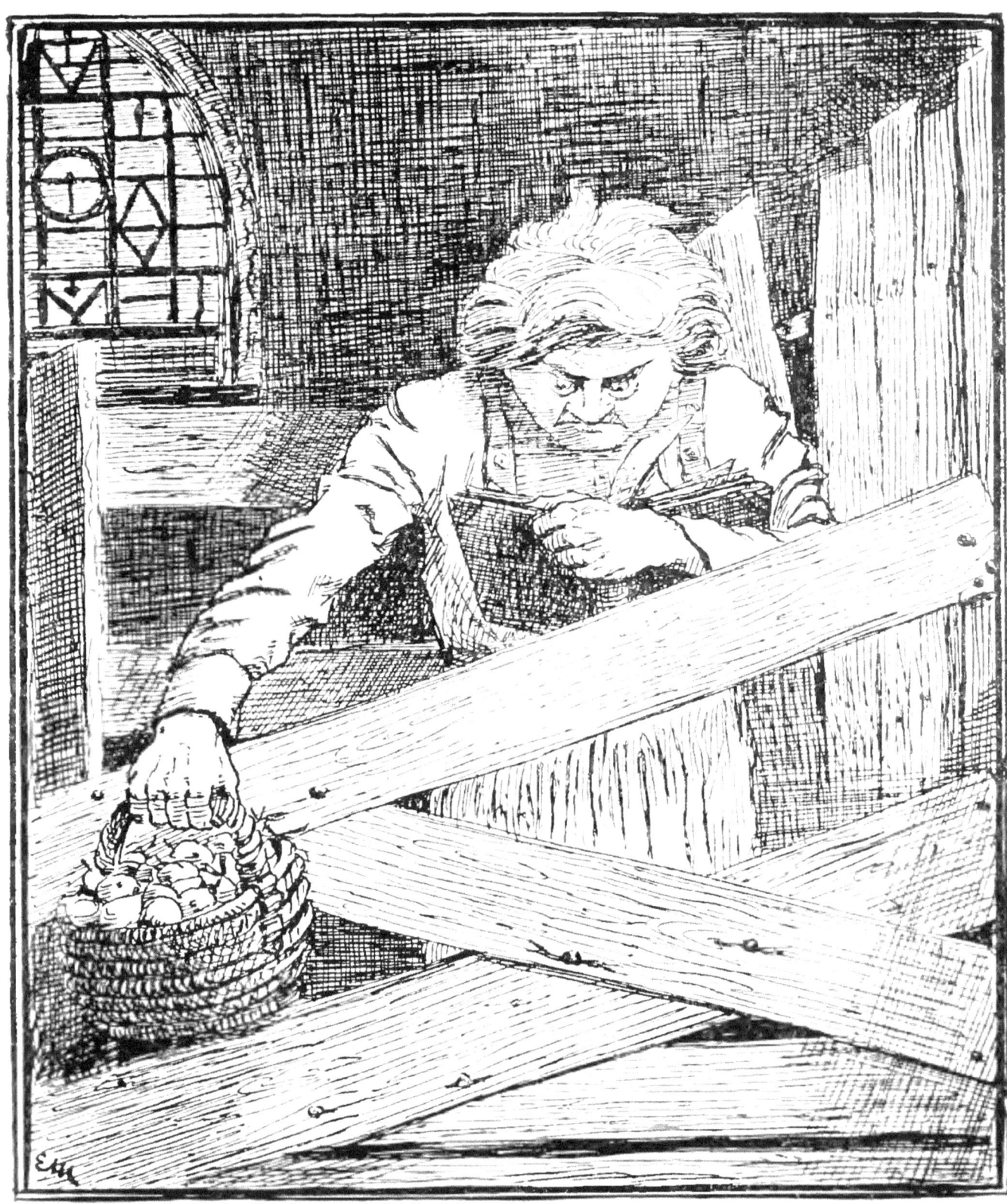

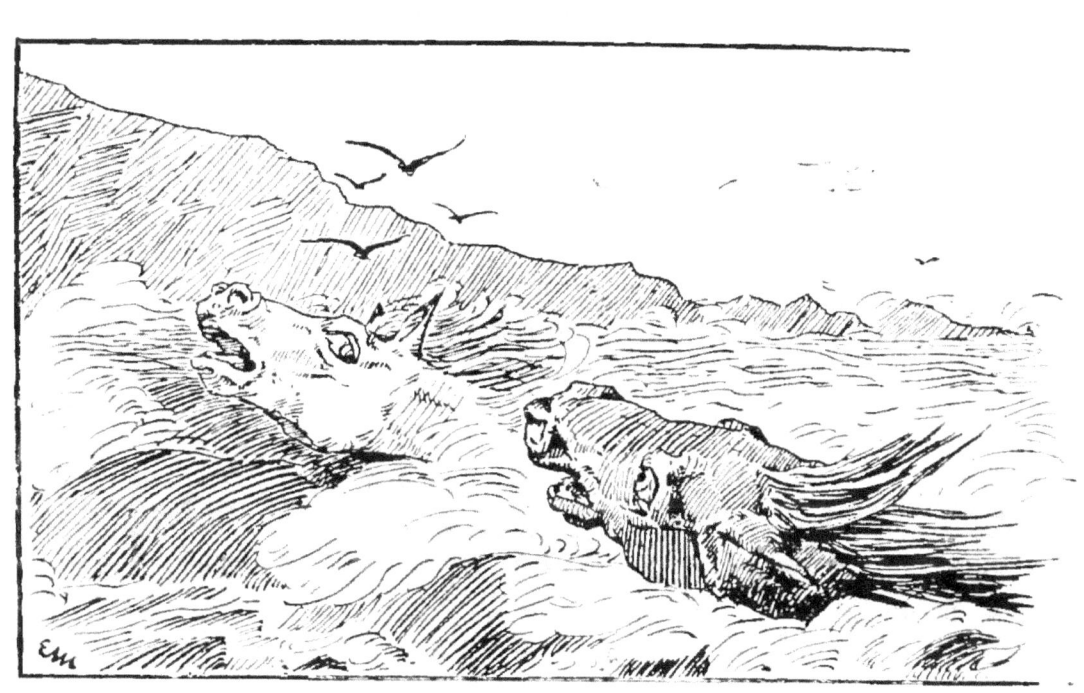

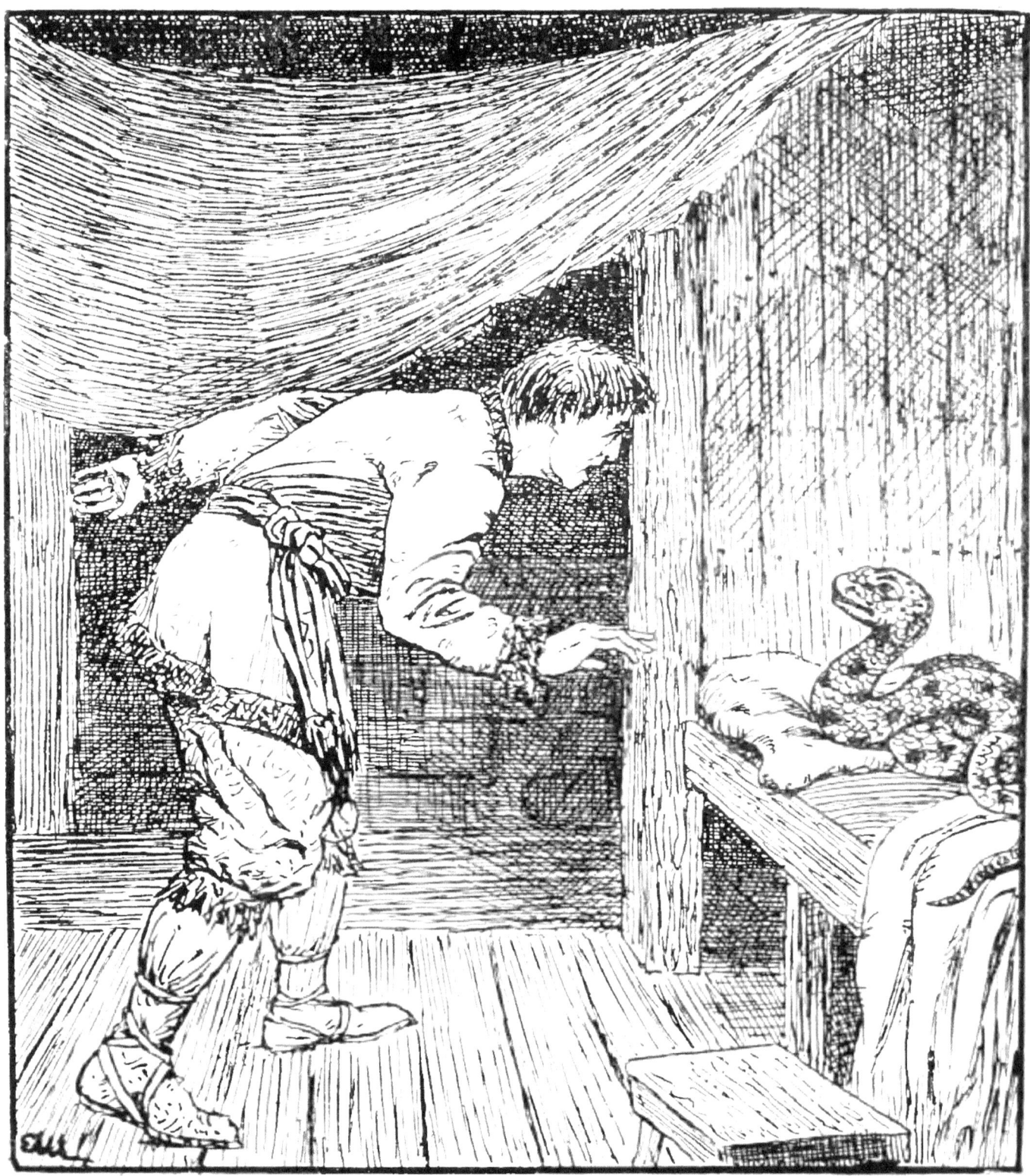

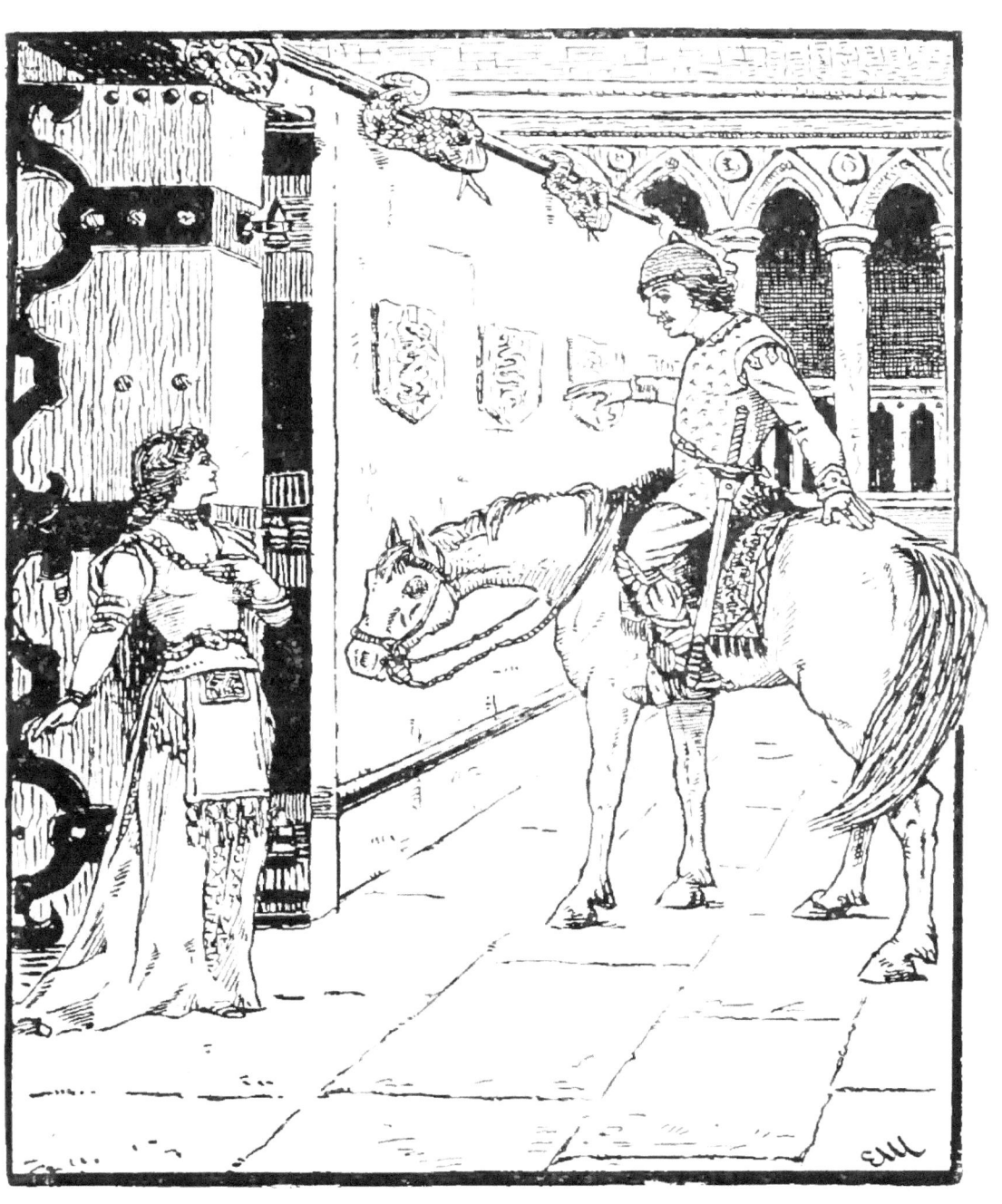

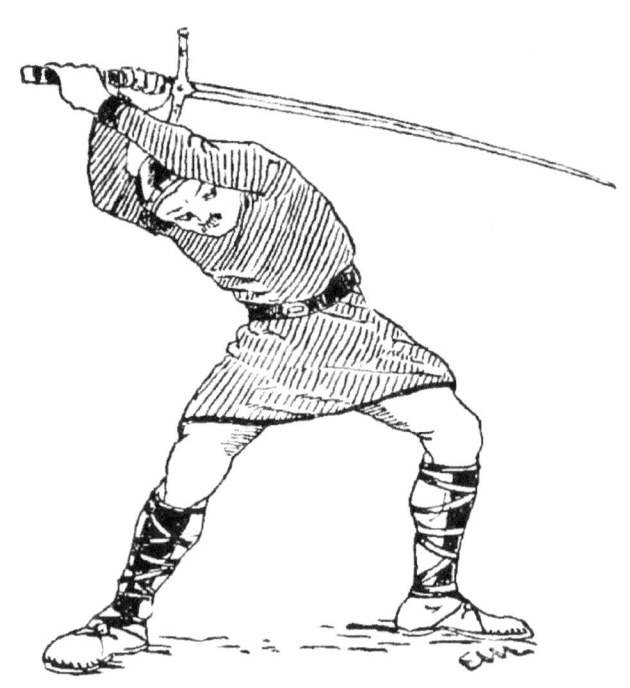

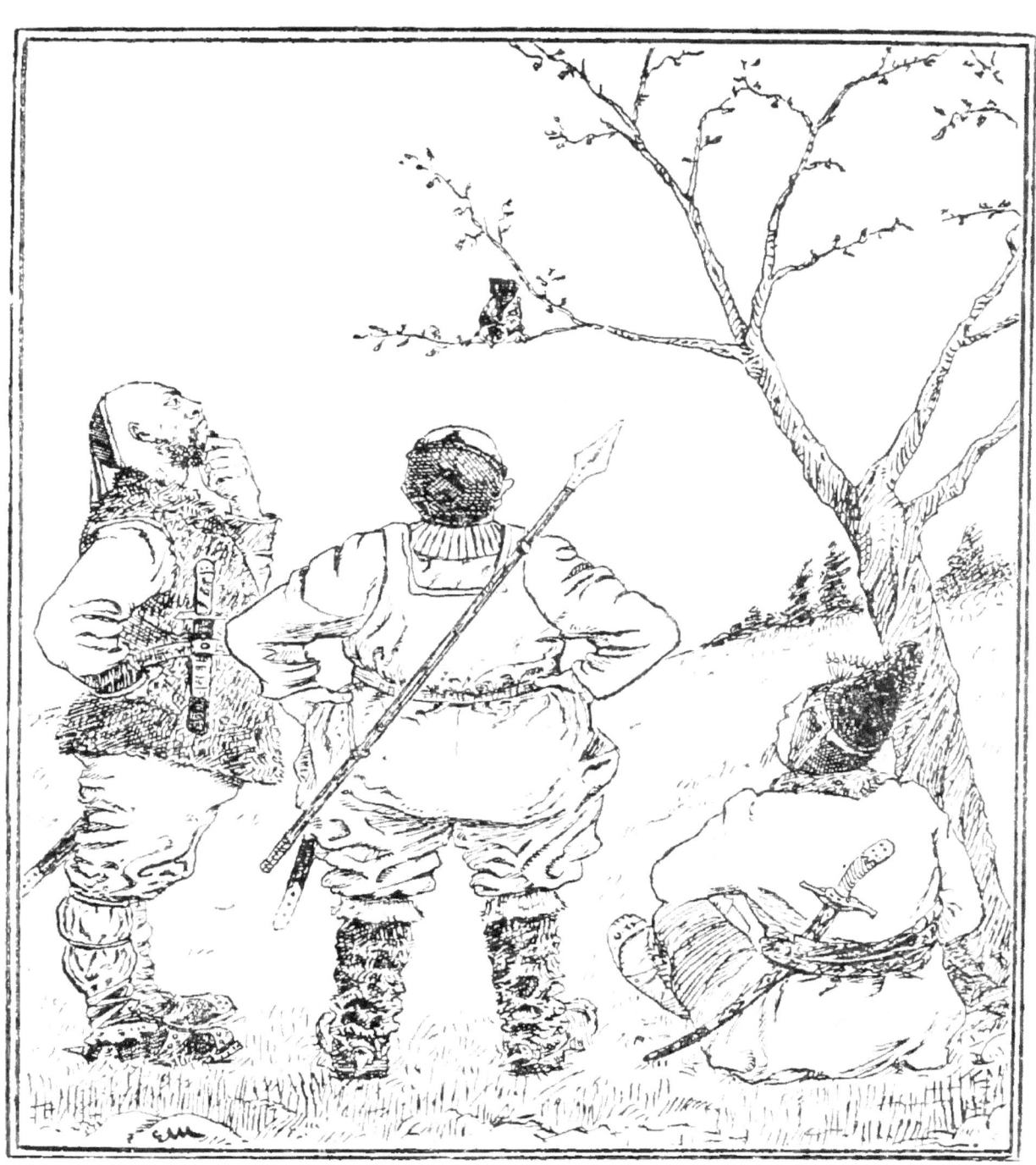

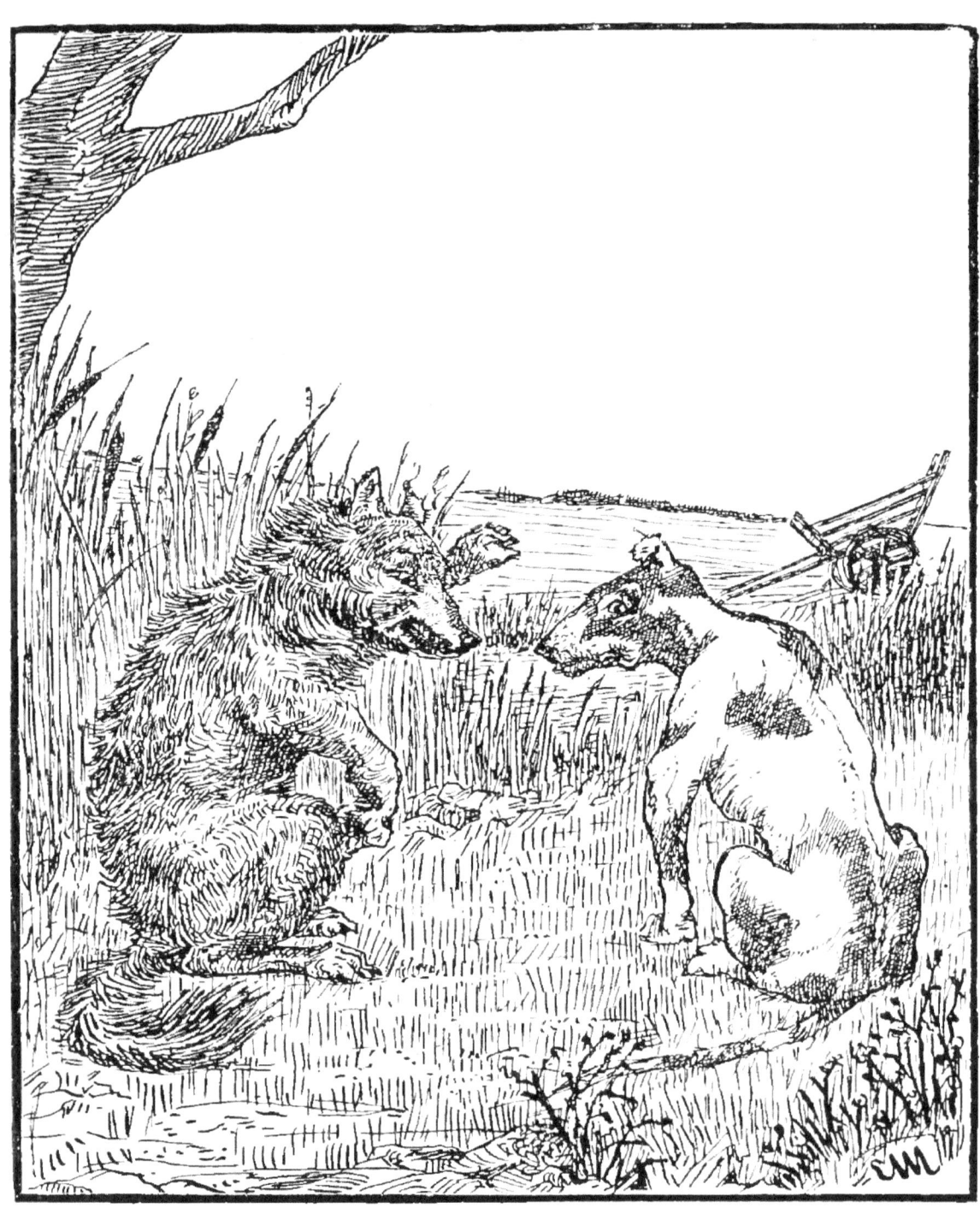

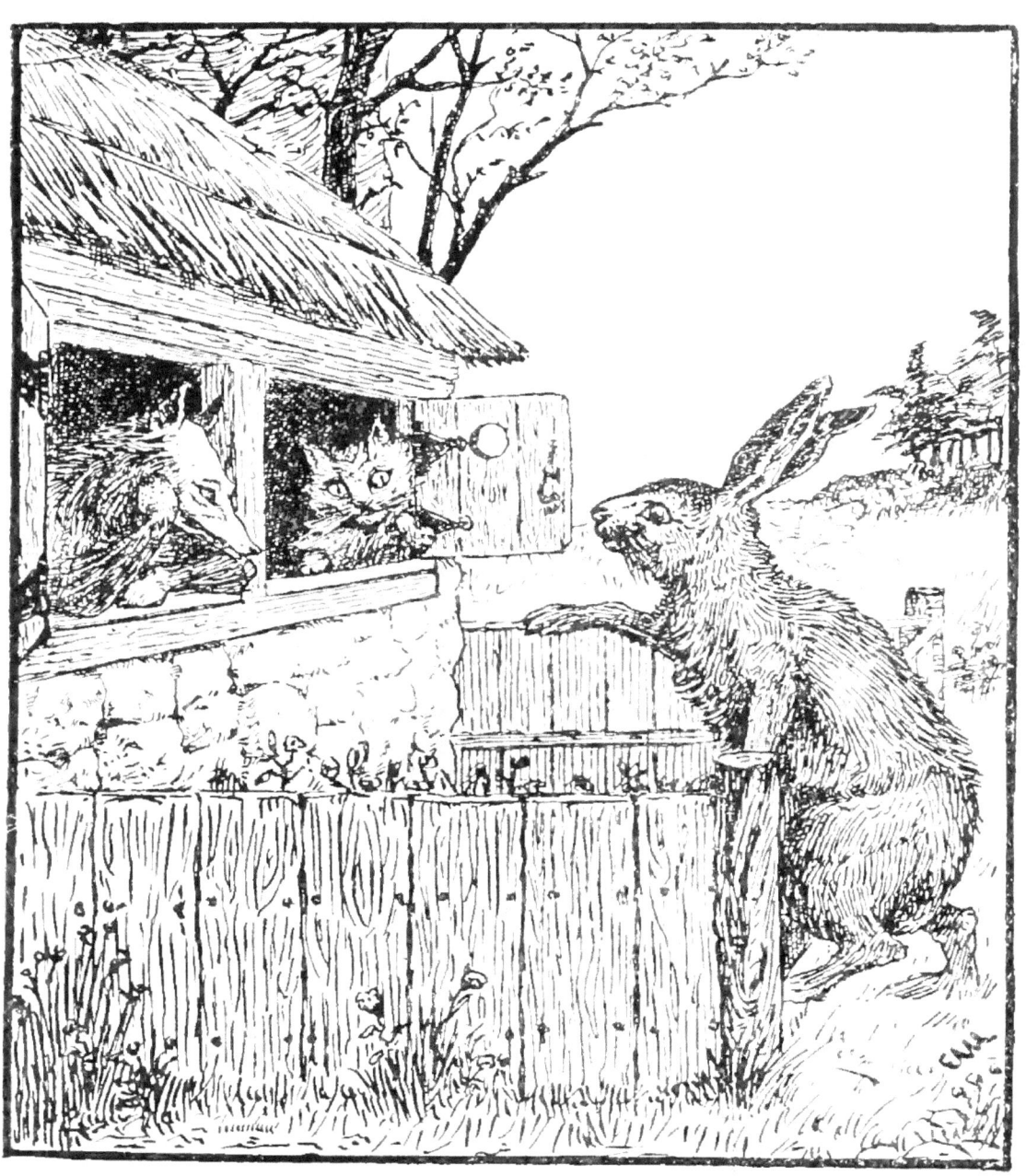

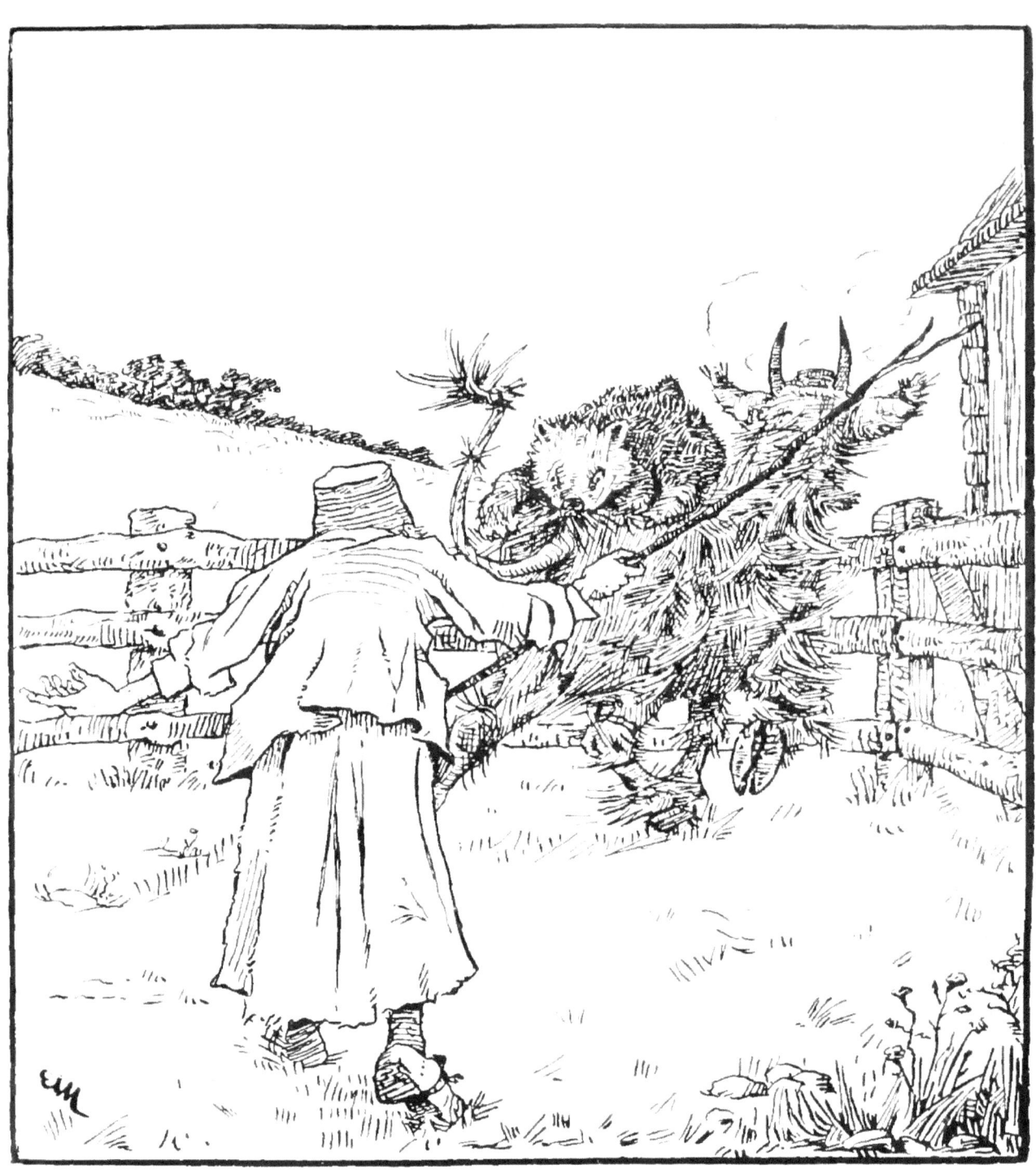

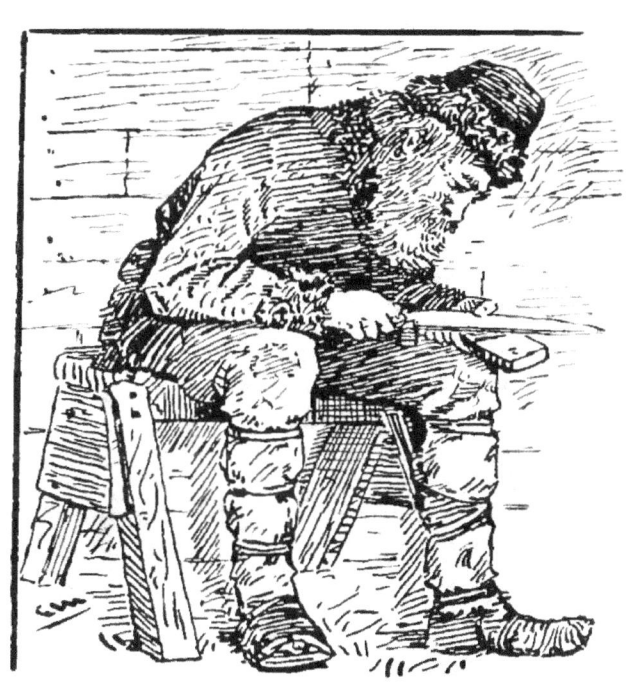

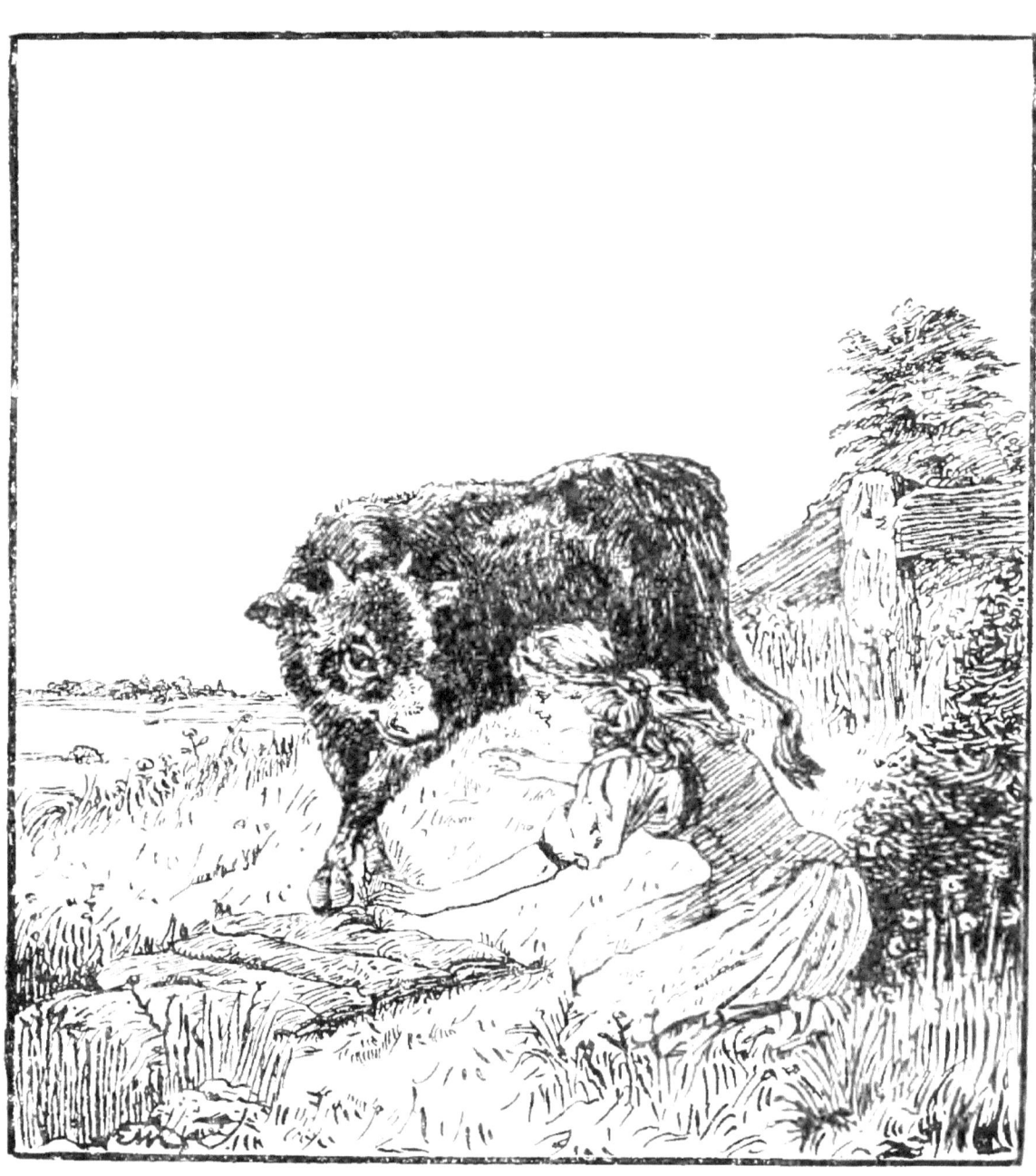

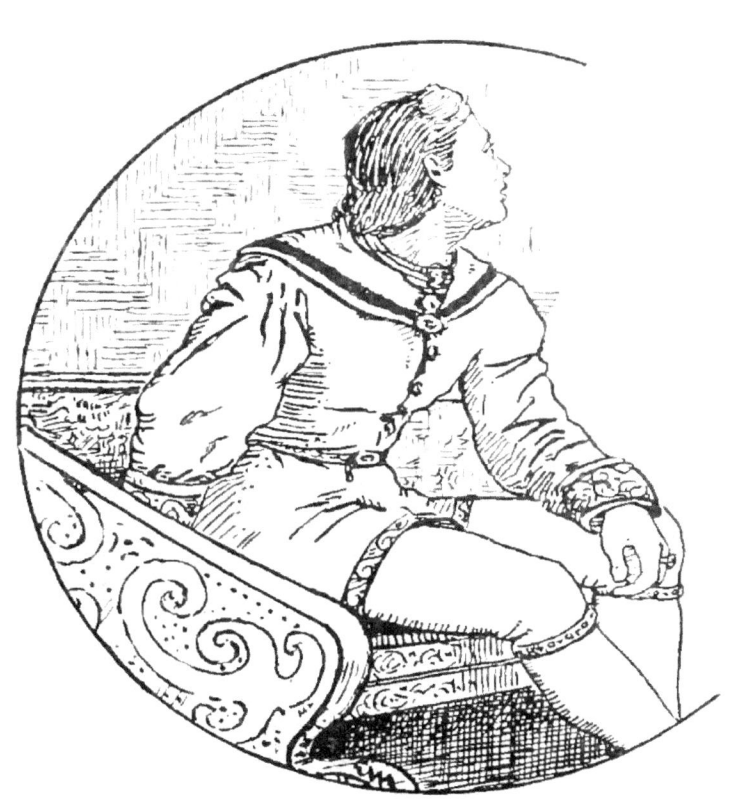

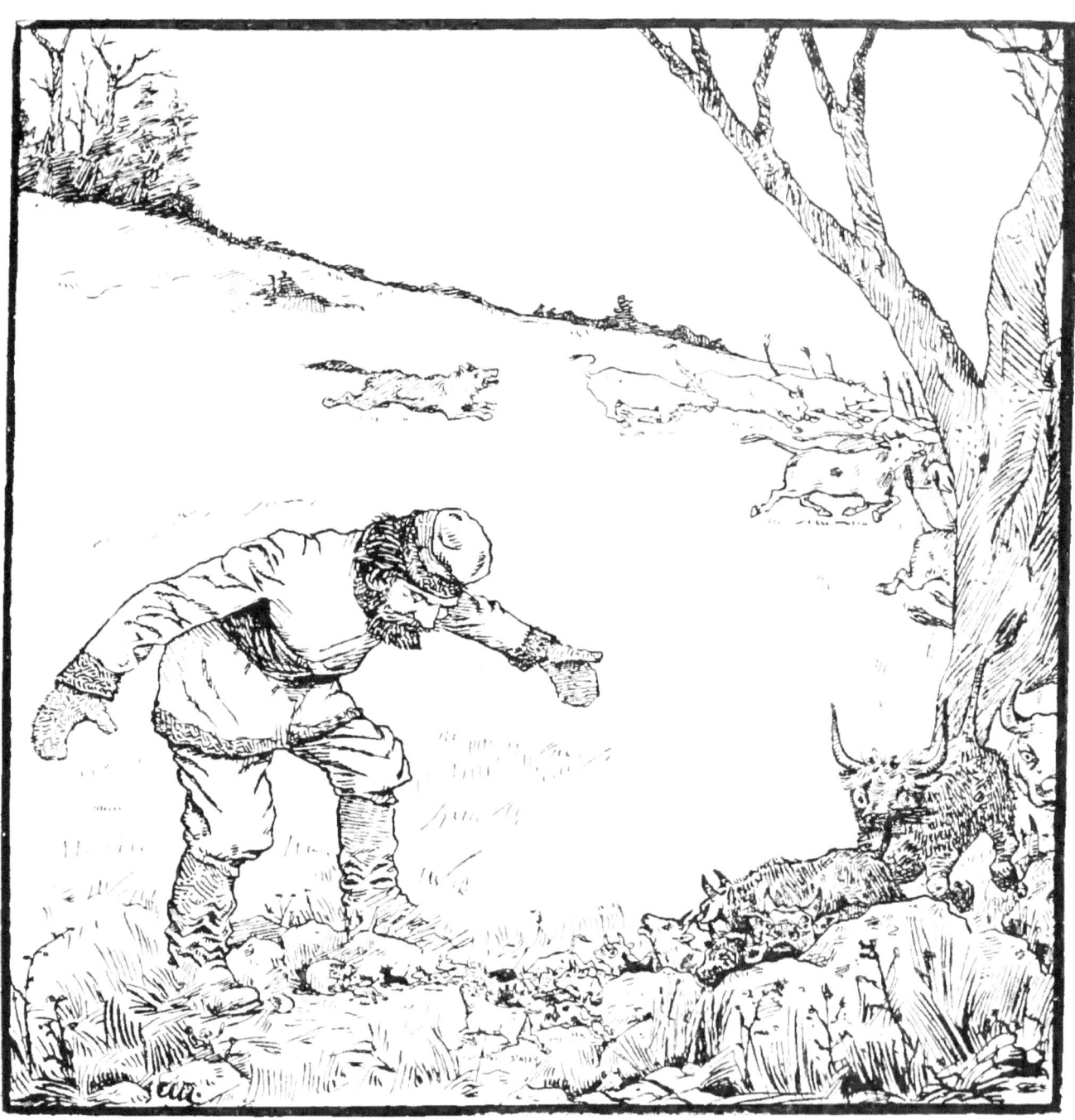

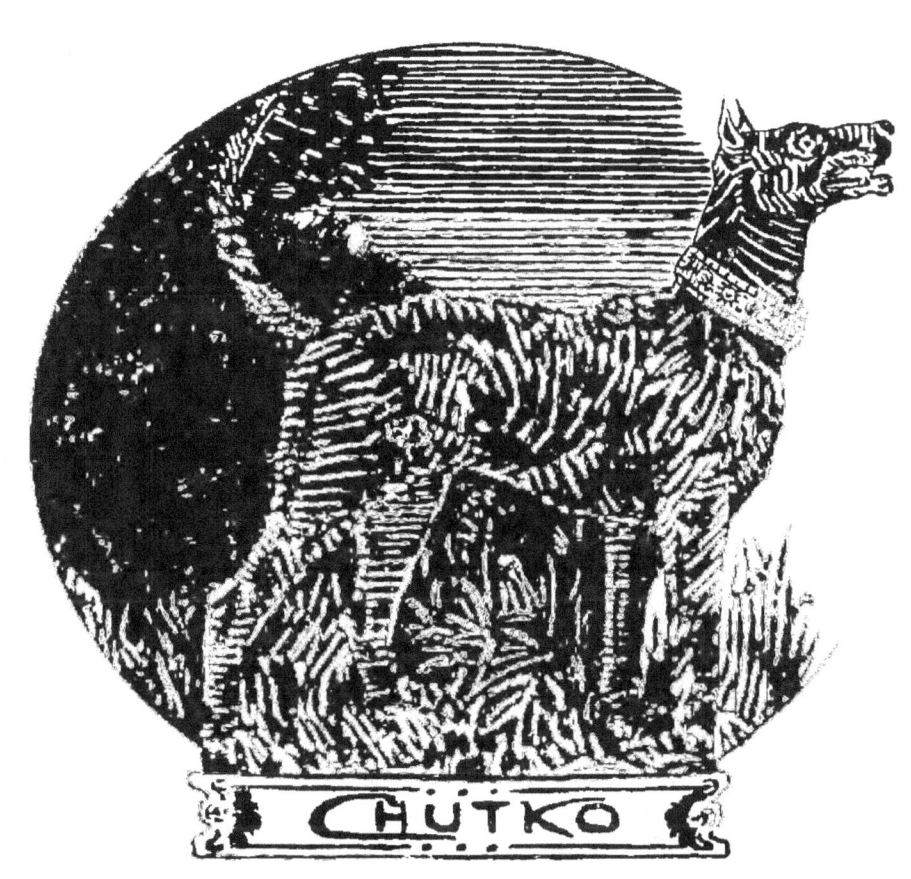

CHUTKO

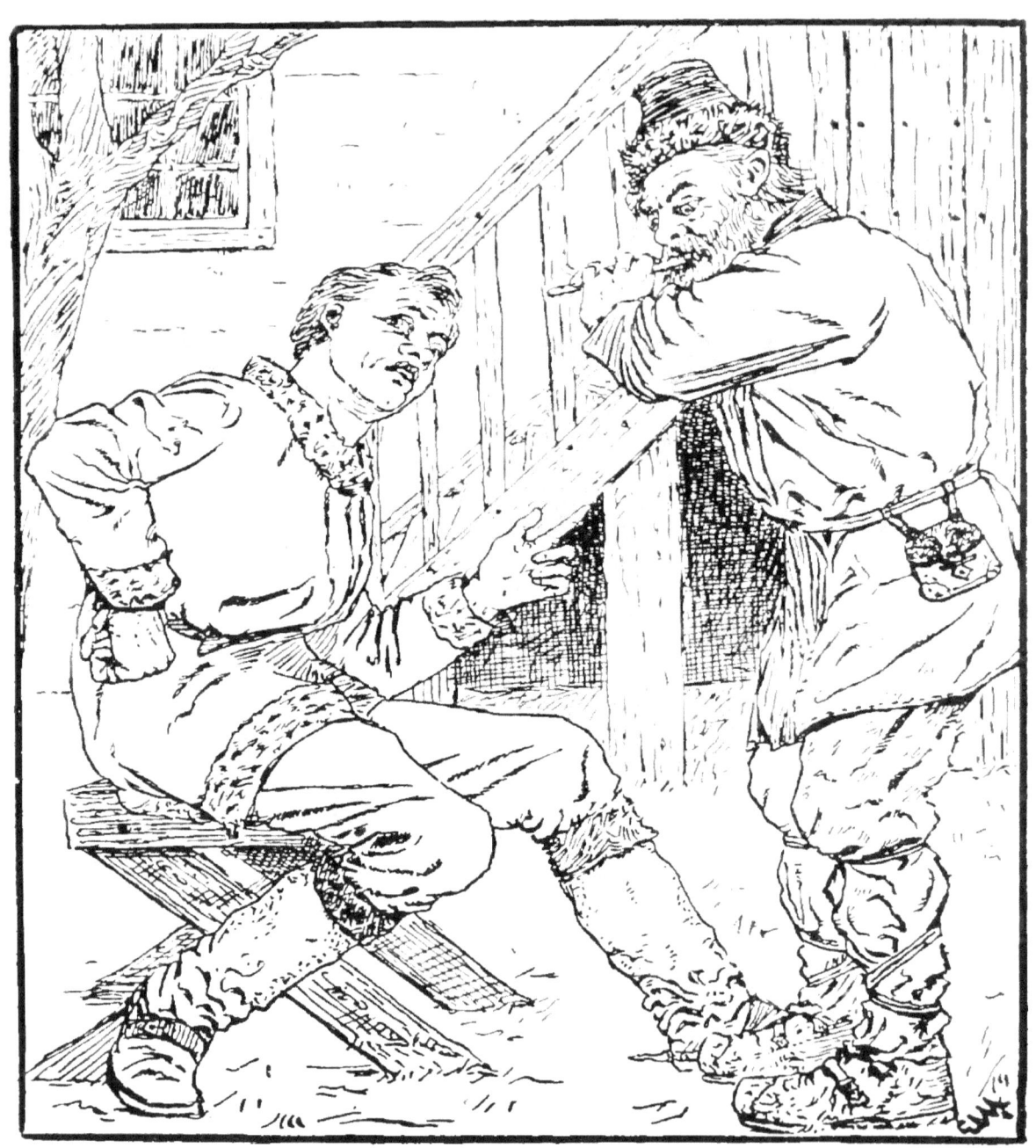

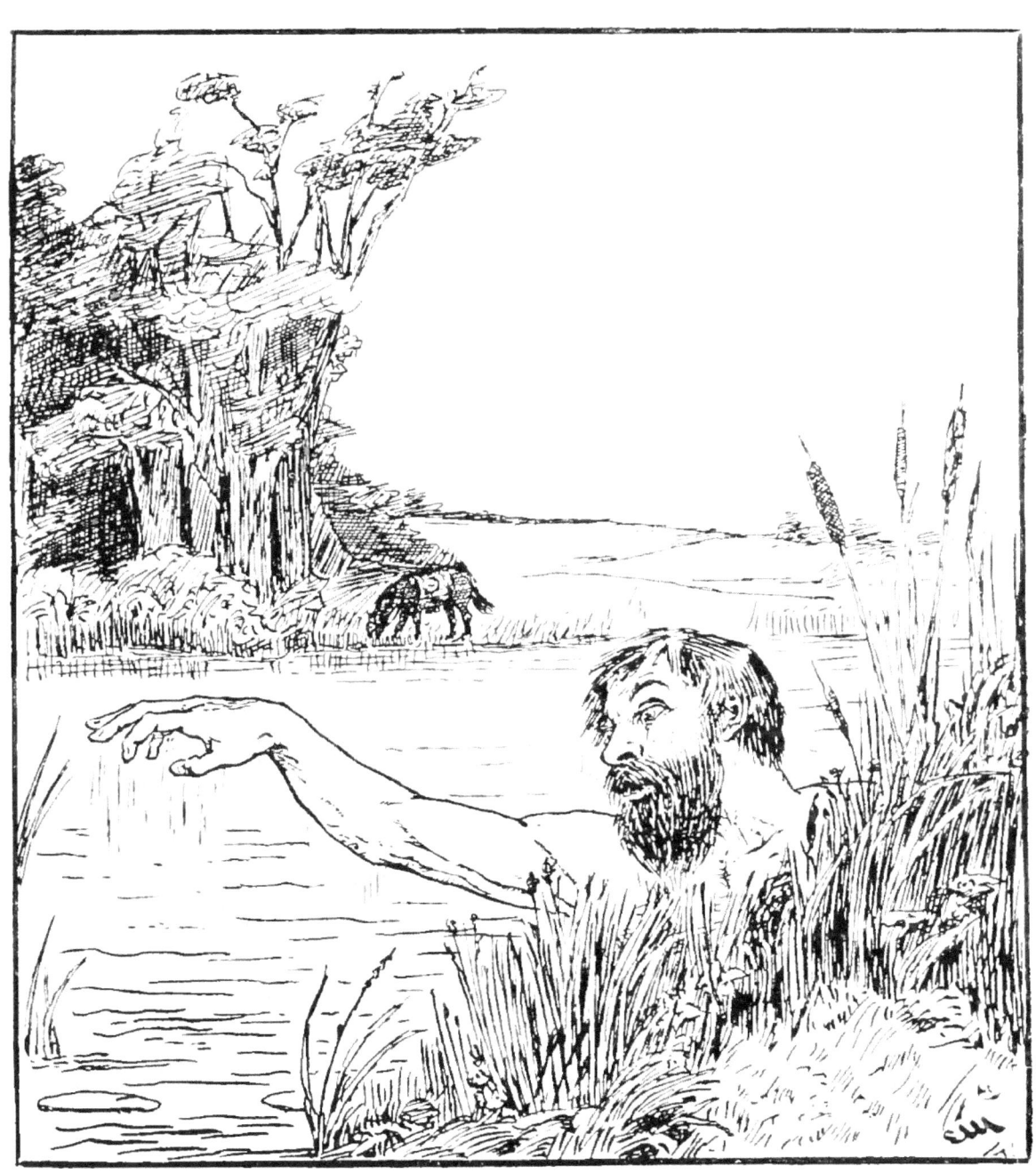

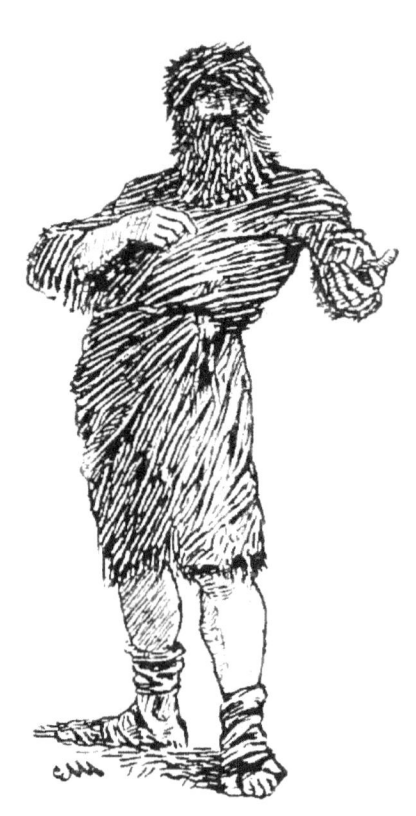

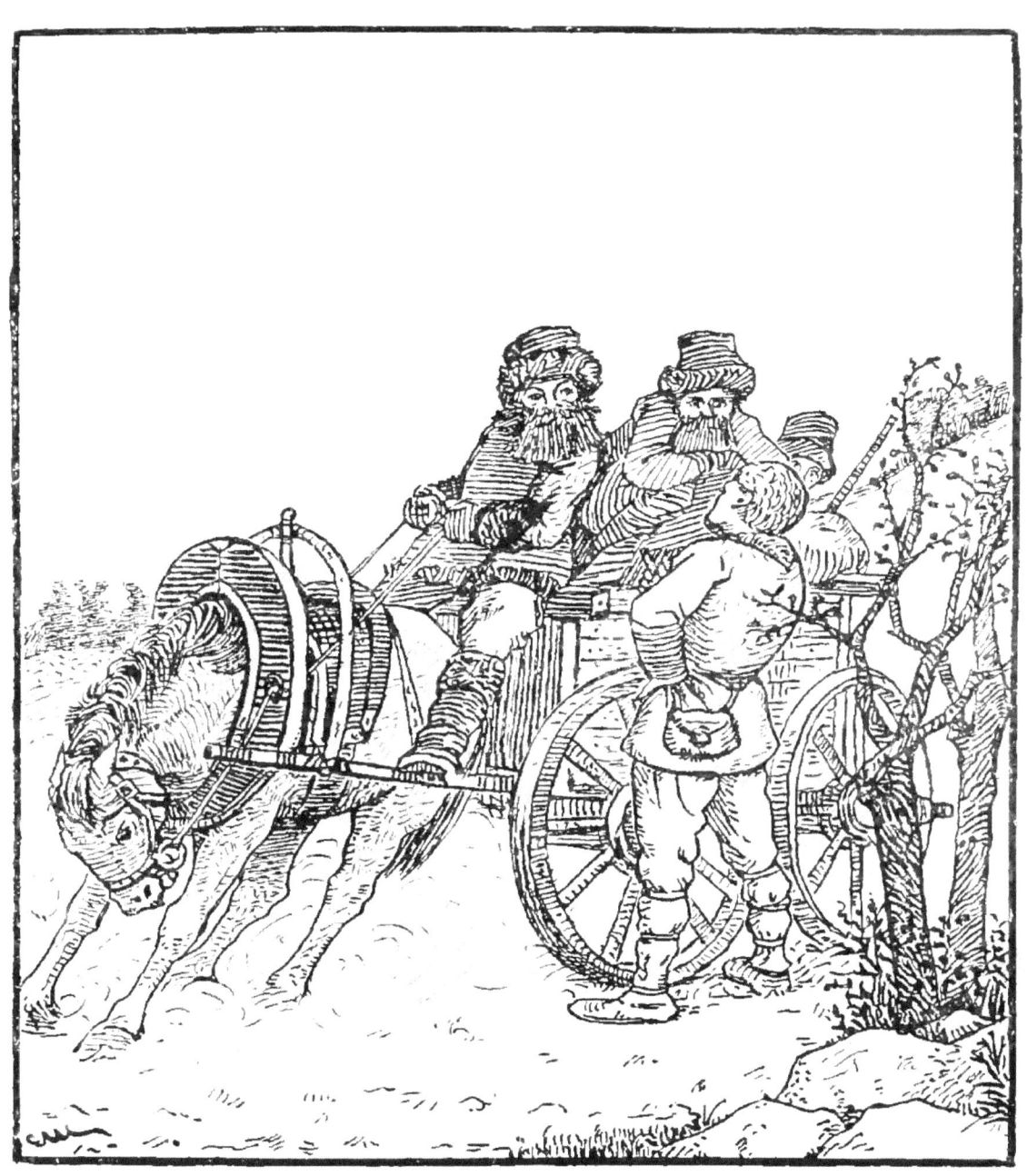

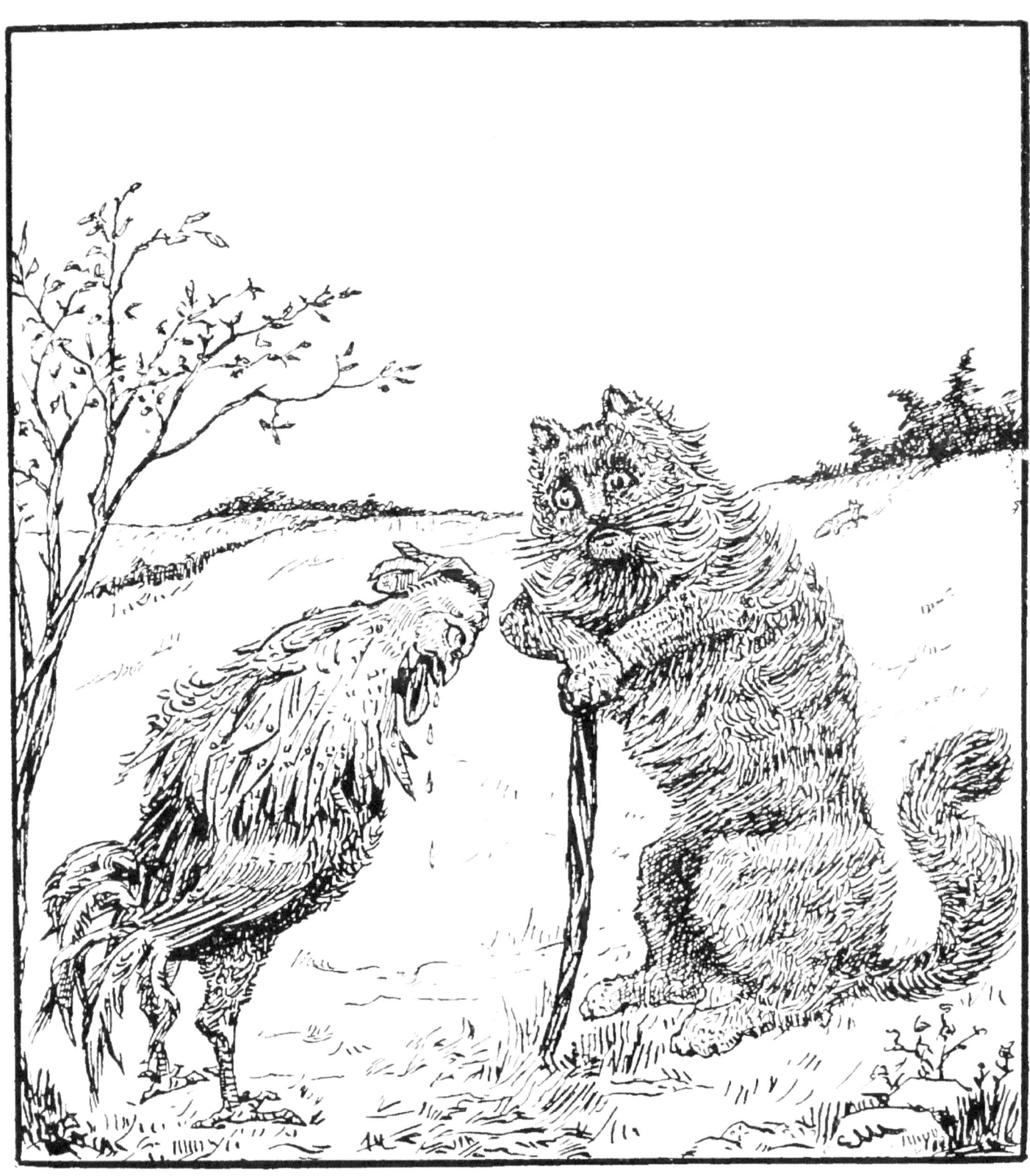

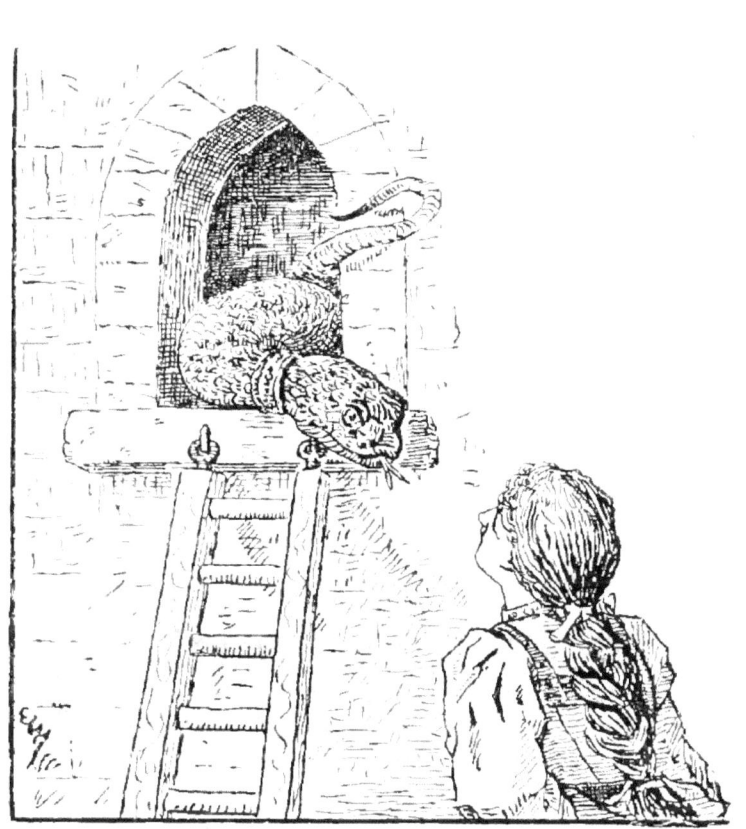

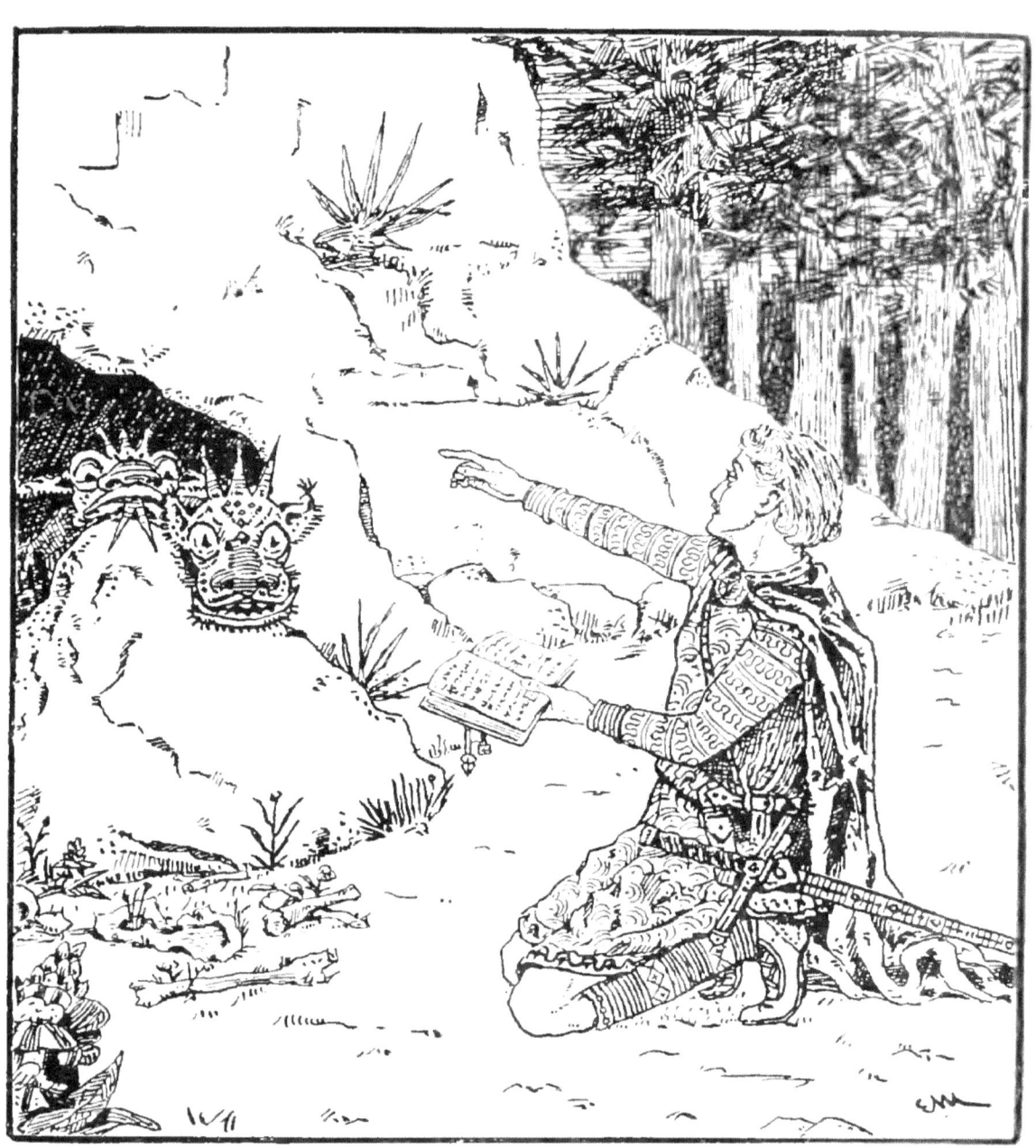

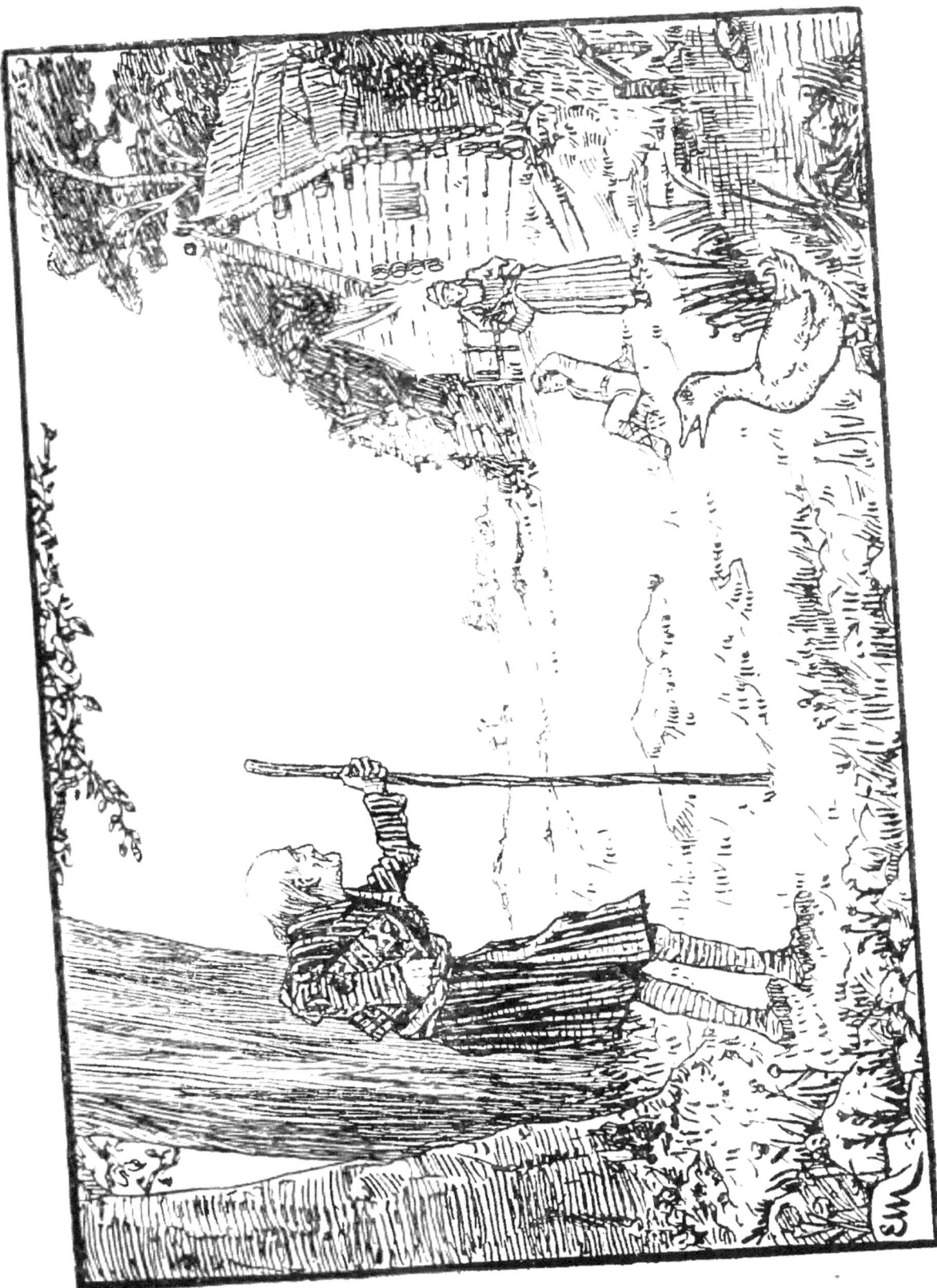

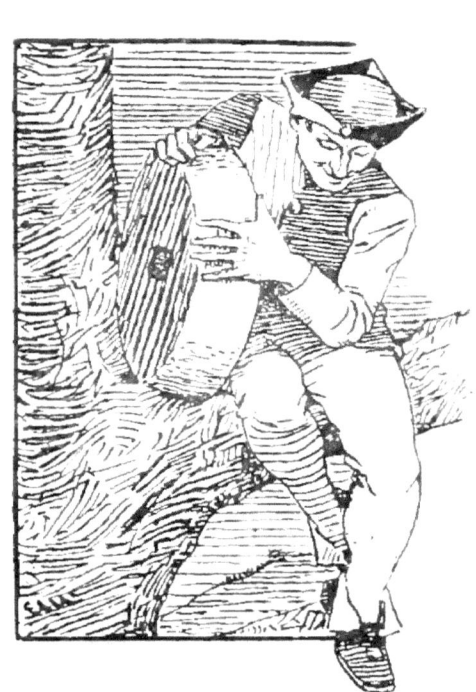

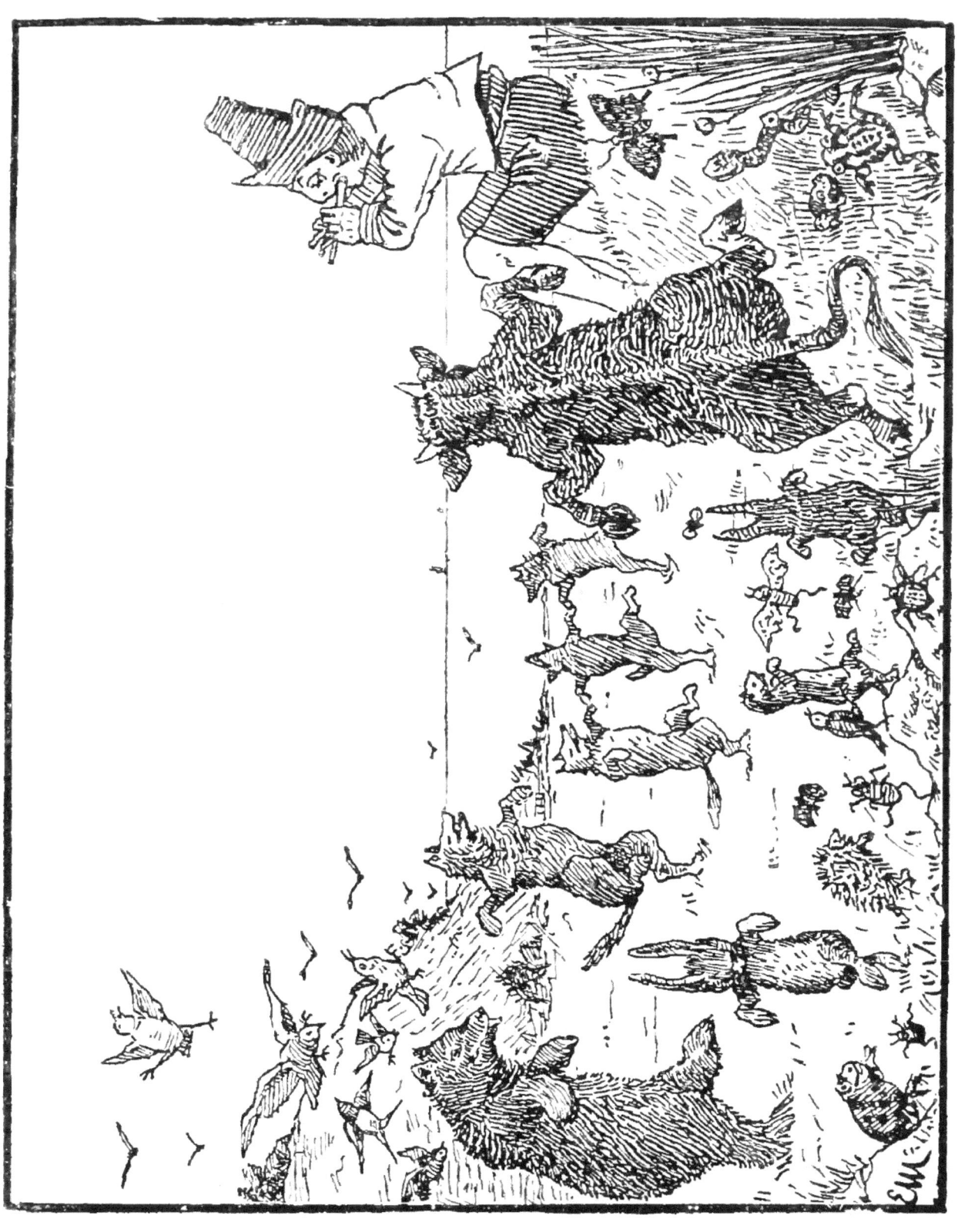

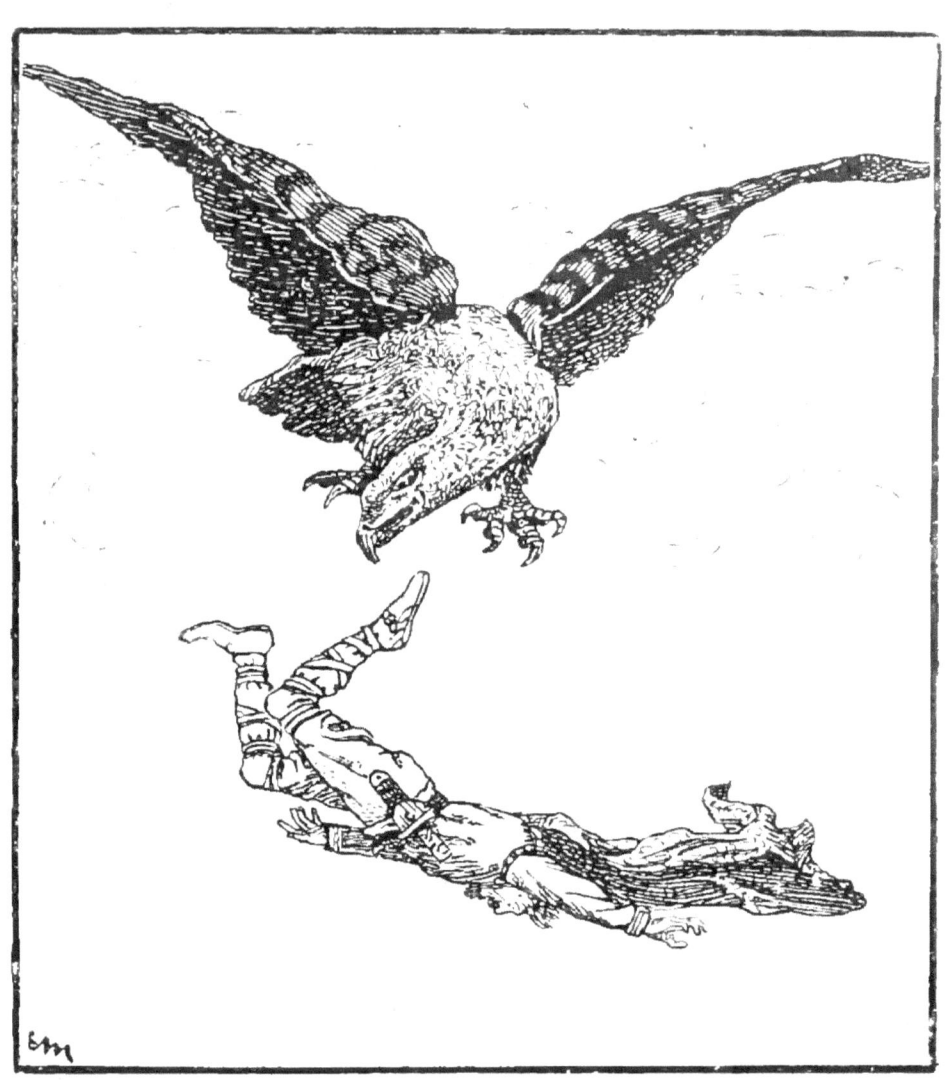

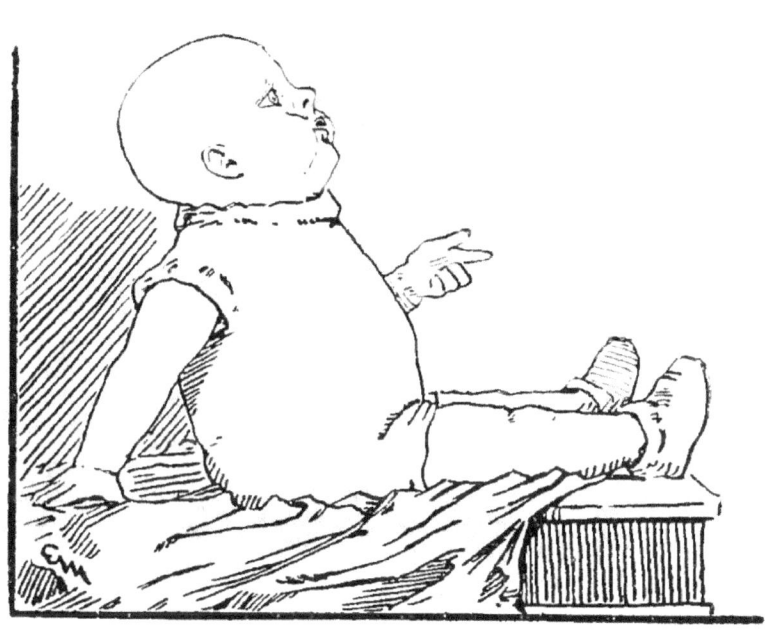

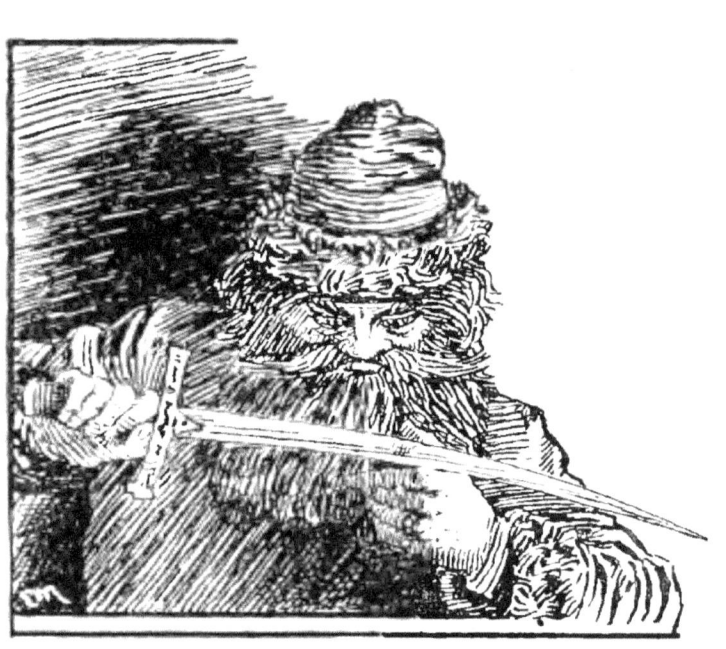

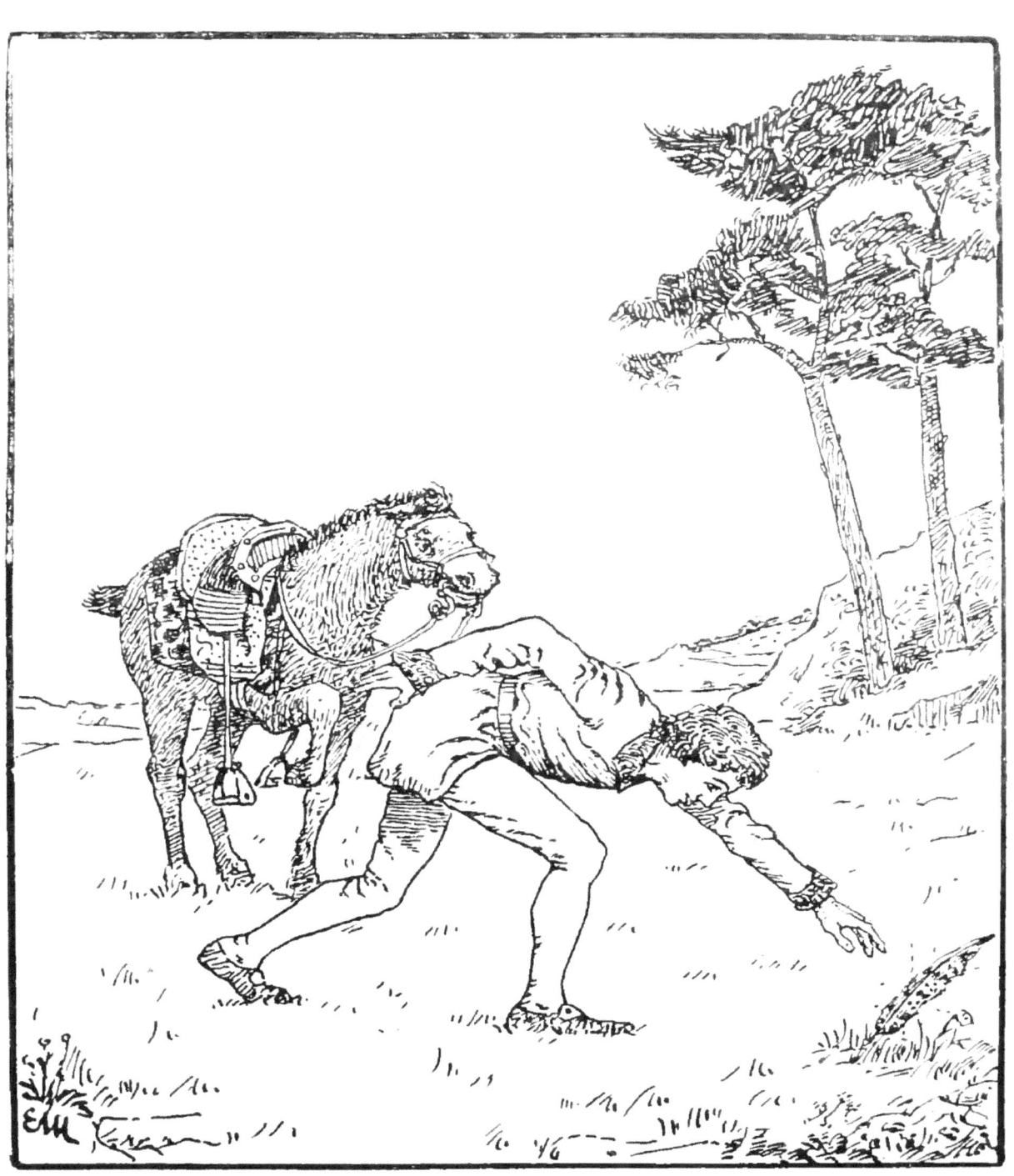

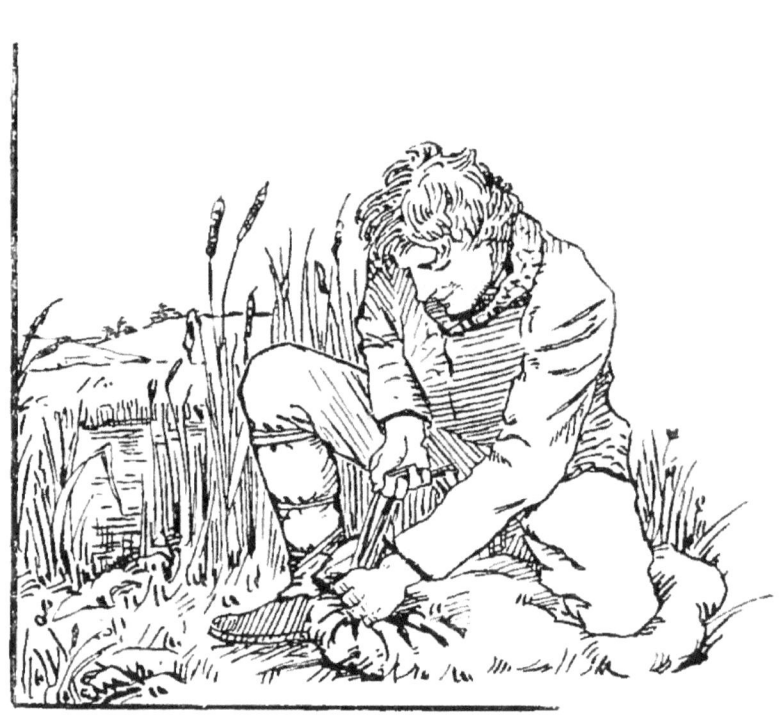

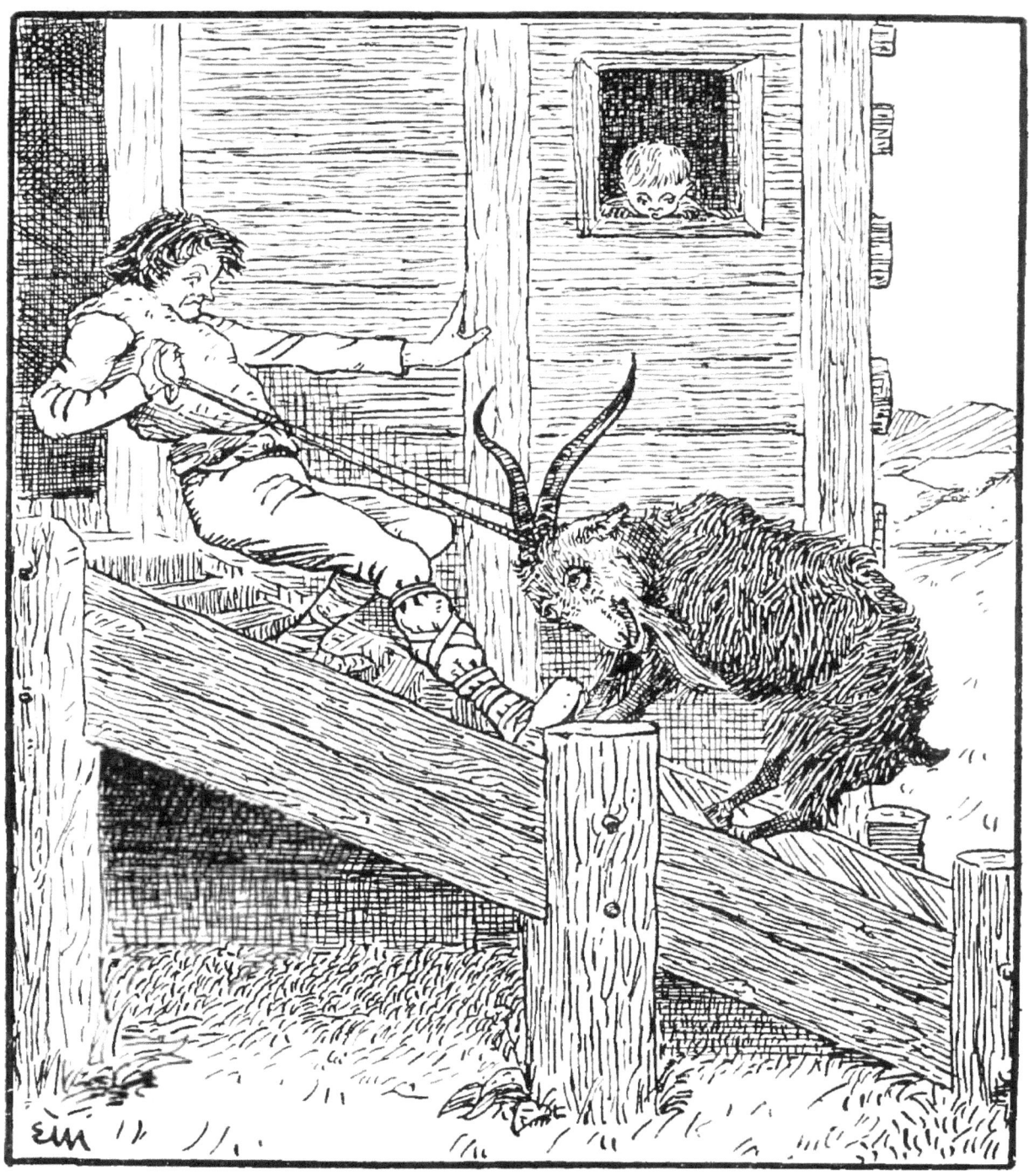

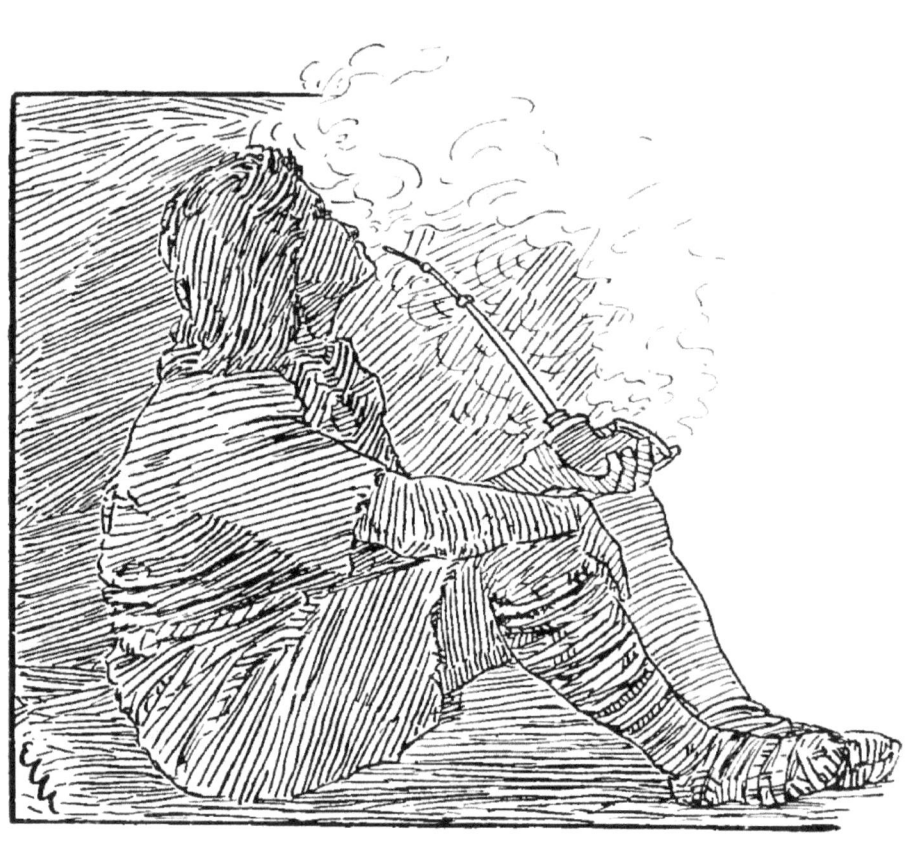

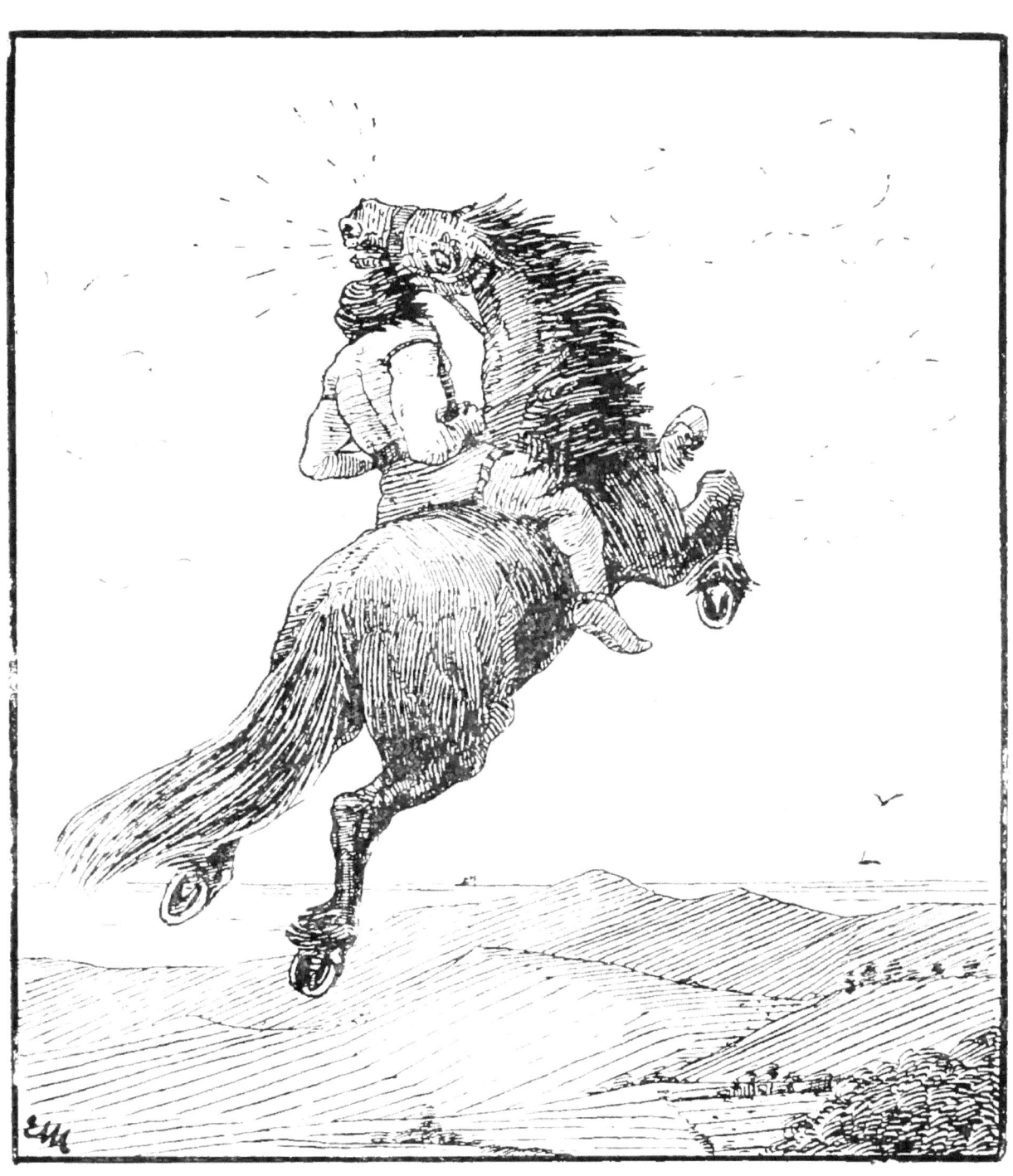

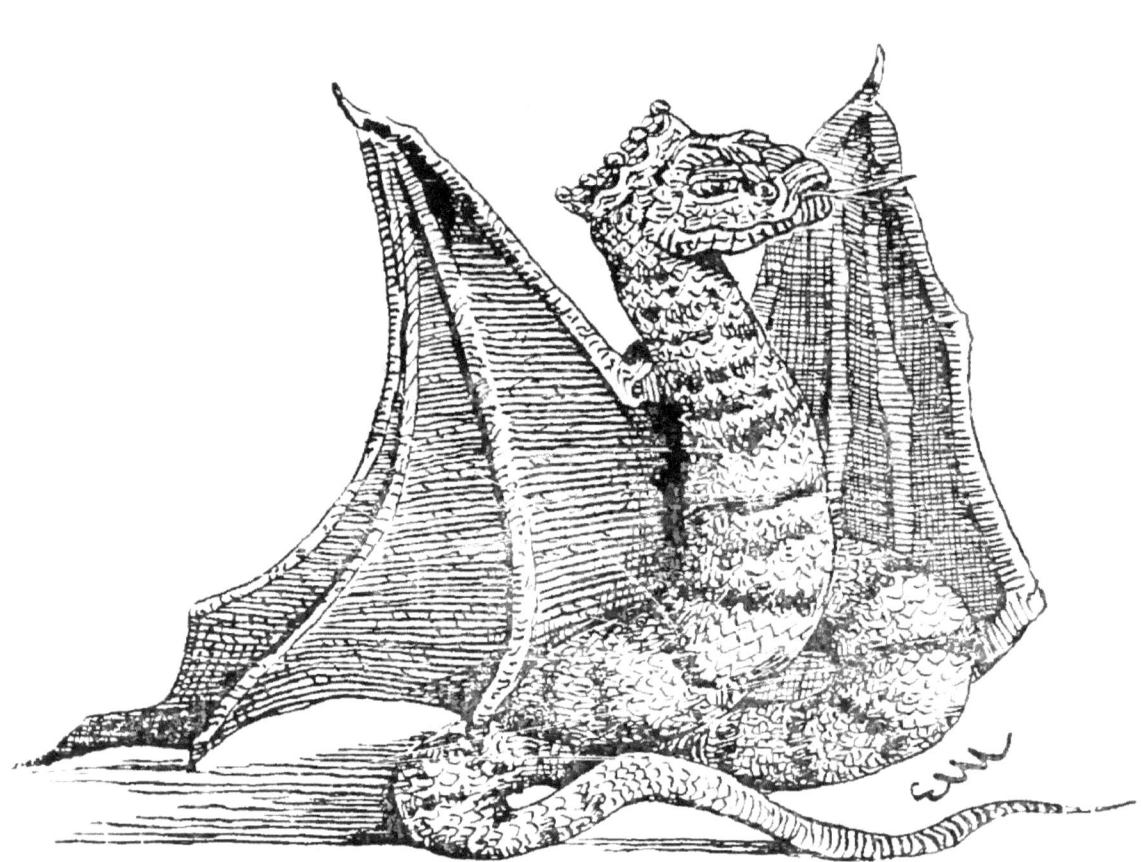

COSSACK
FAIRY TALES
AND FOLK TALES

ILLUSTRATED BY
NOEL L. NISBET

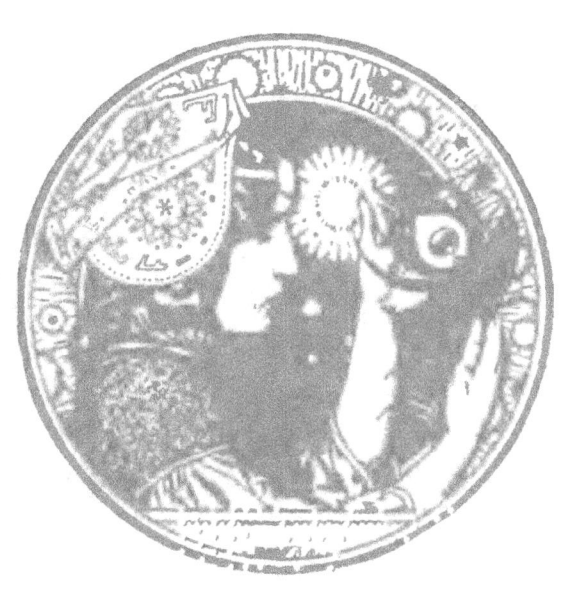

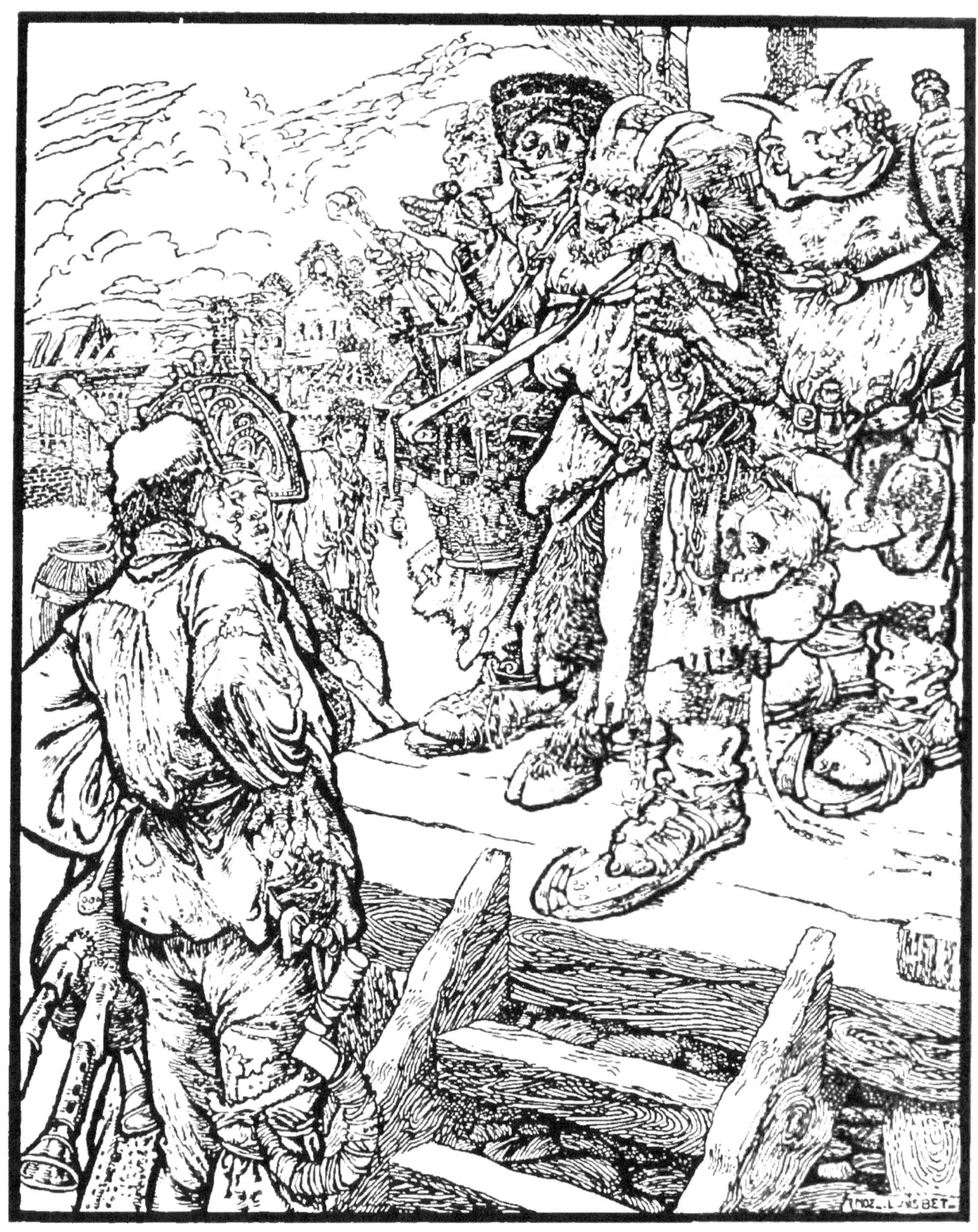

ALL MANNER OF EVIL POWERS WALKED ABROAD

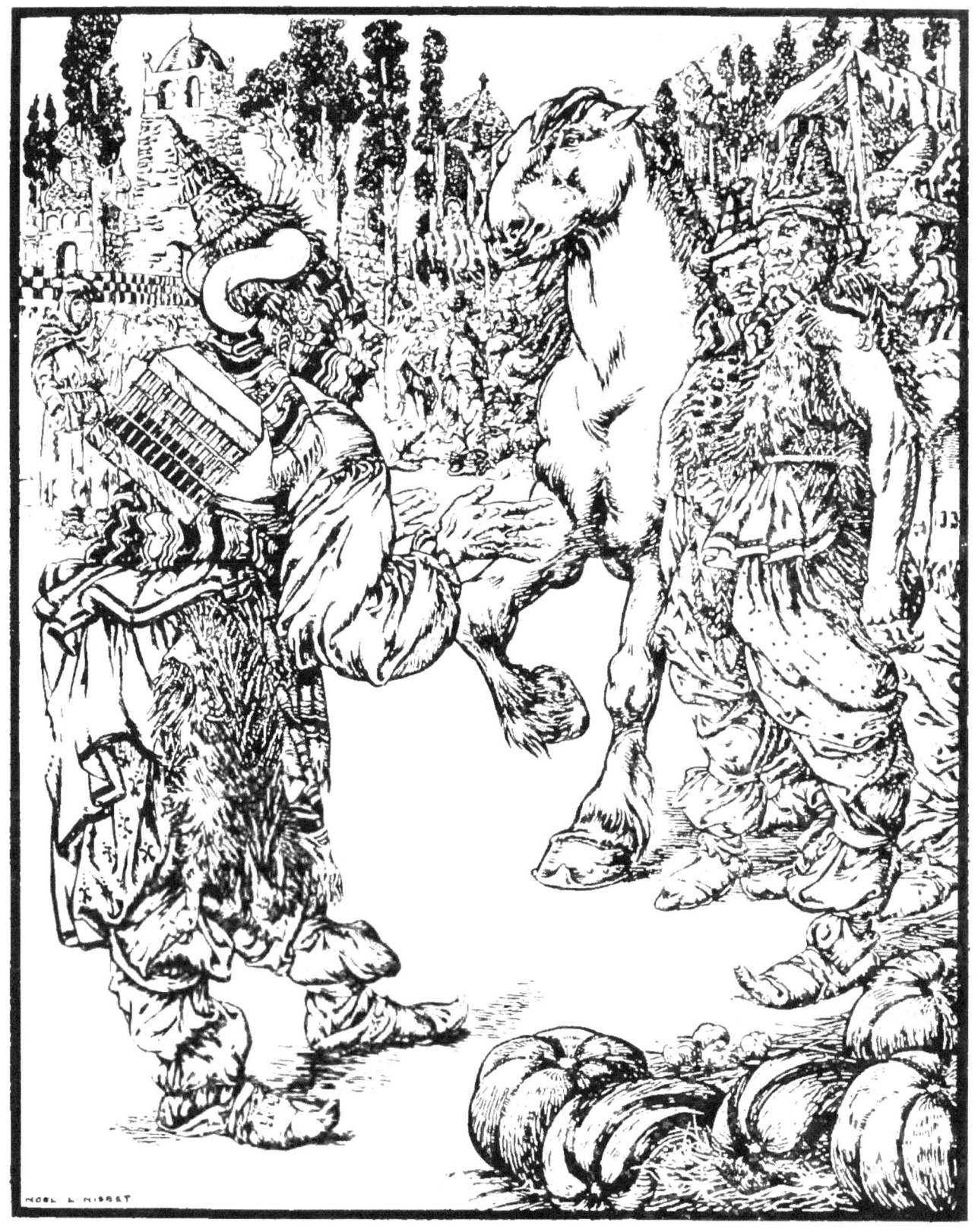

"HOW MUCH DO YOU WANT FOR THAT HORSE?"

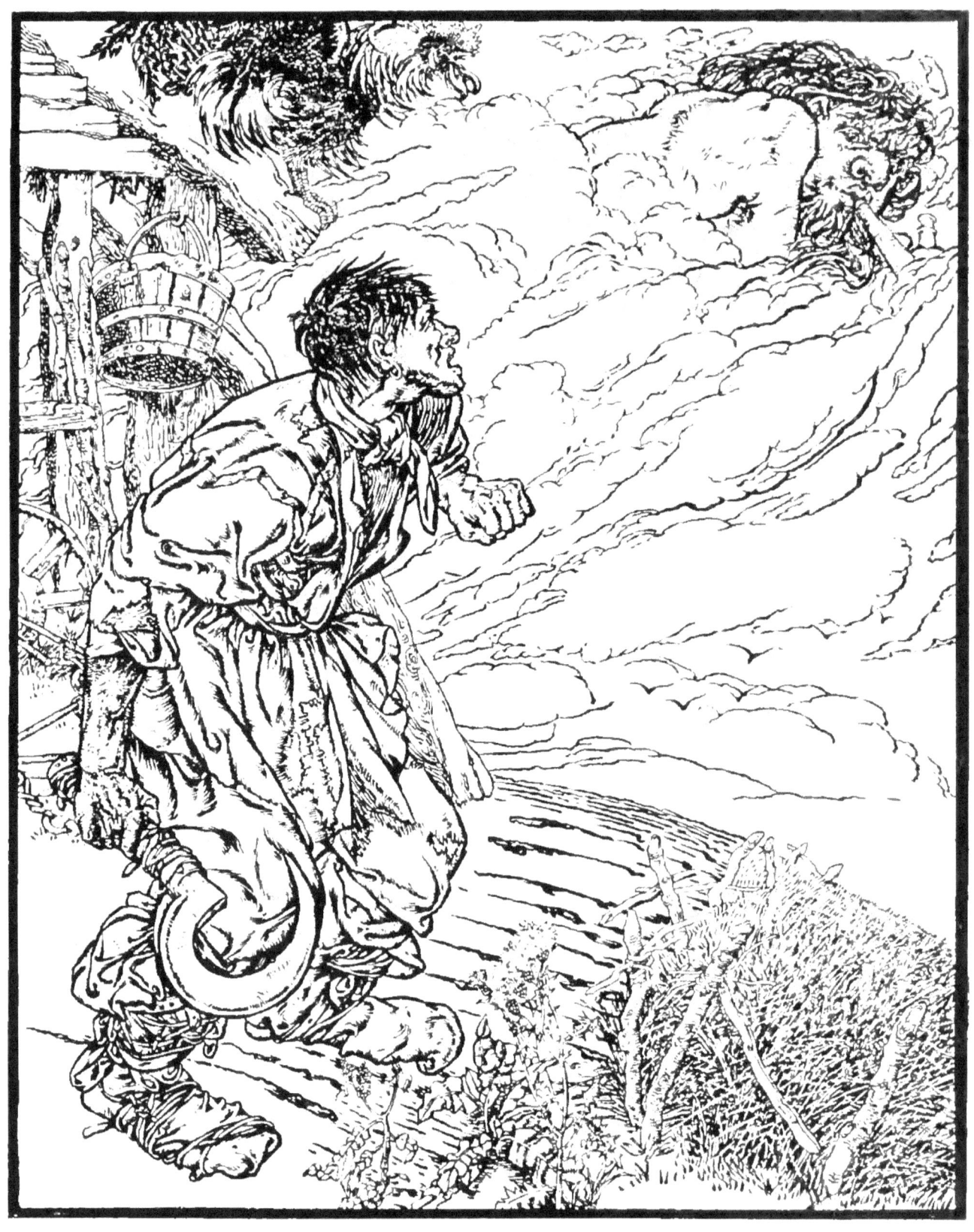

THE WIND CAME AND SWEPT ALL HIS CORN AWAY

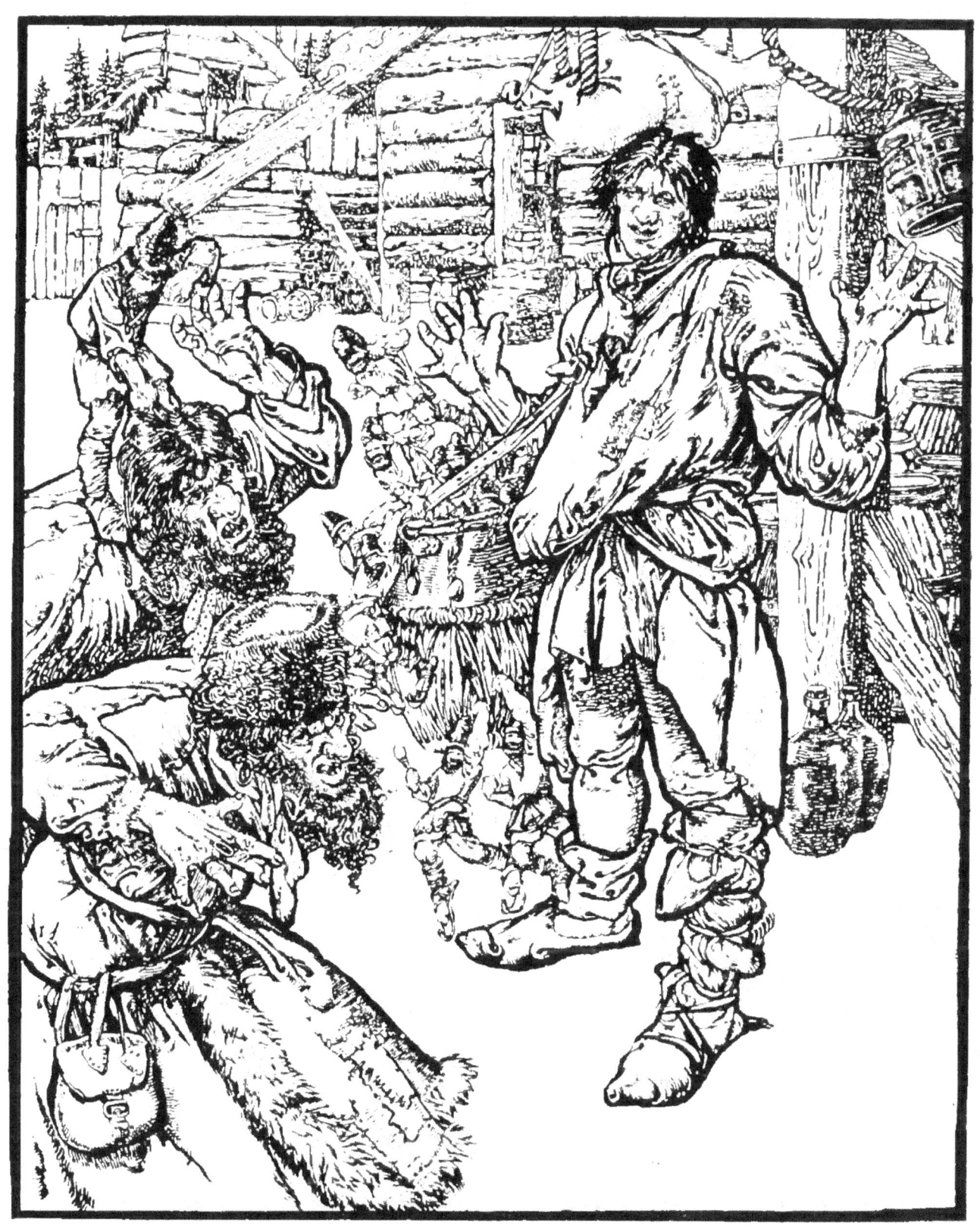

"OUT OF THE DRUM, MY HENCHMEN!"

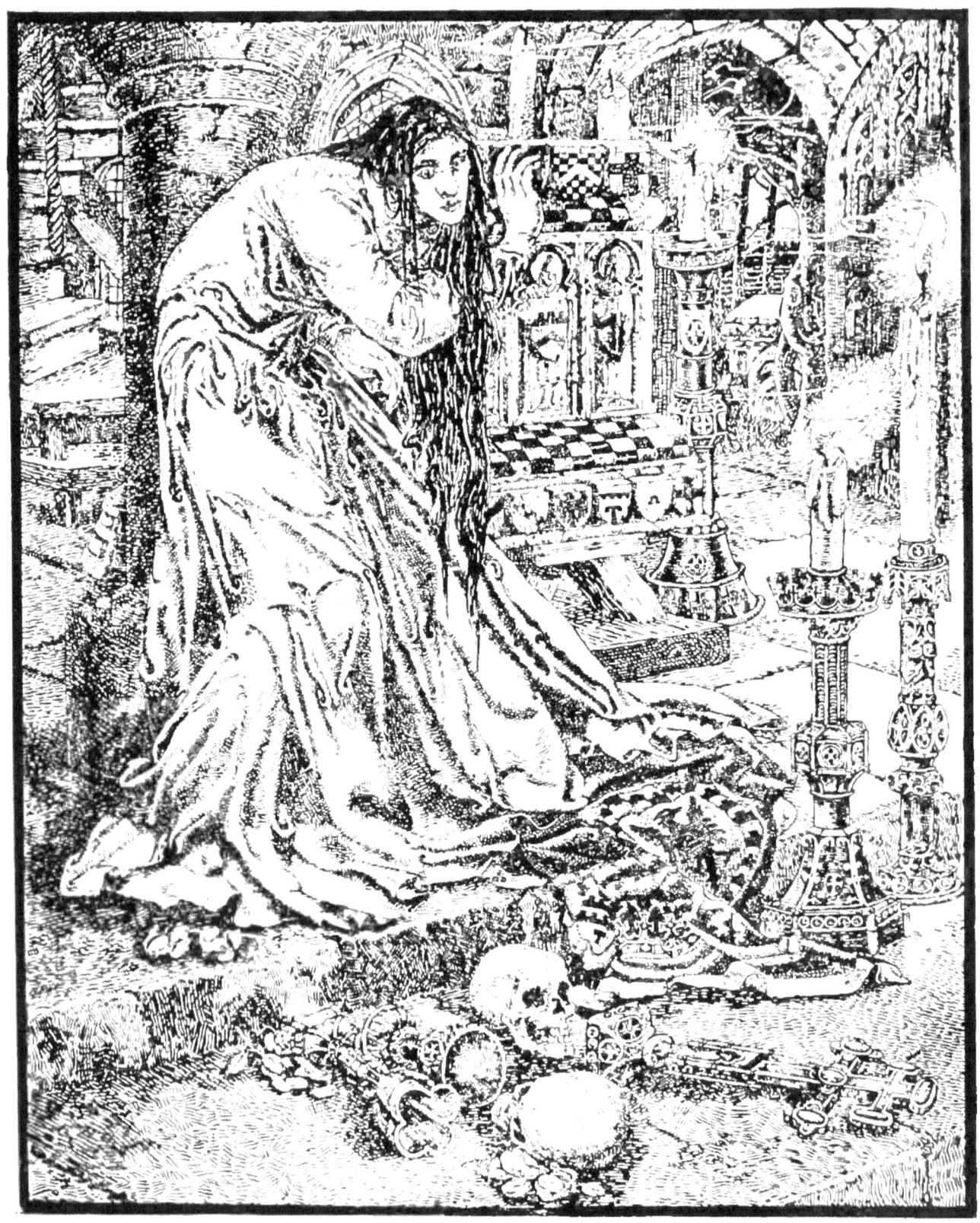

THE TSARIVNA AROSE FROM HER COFFIN

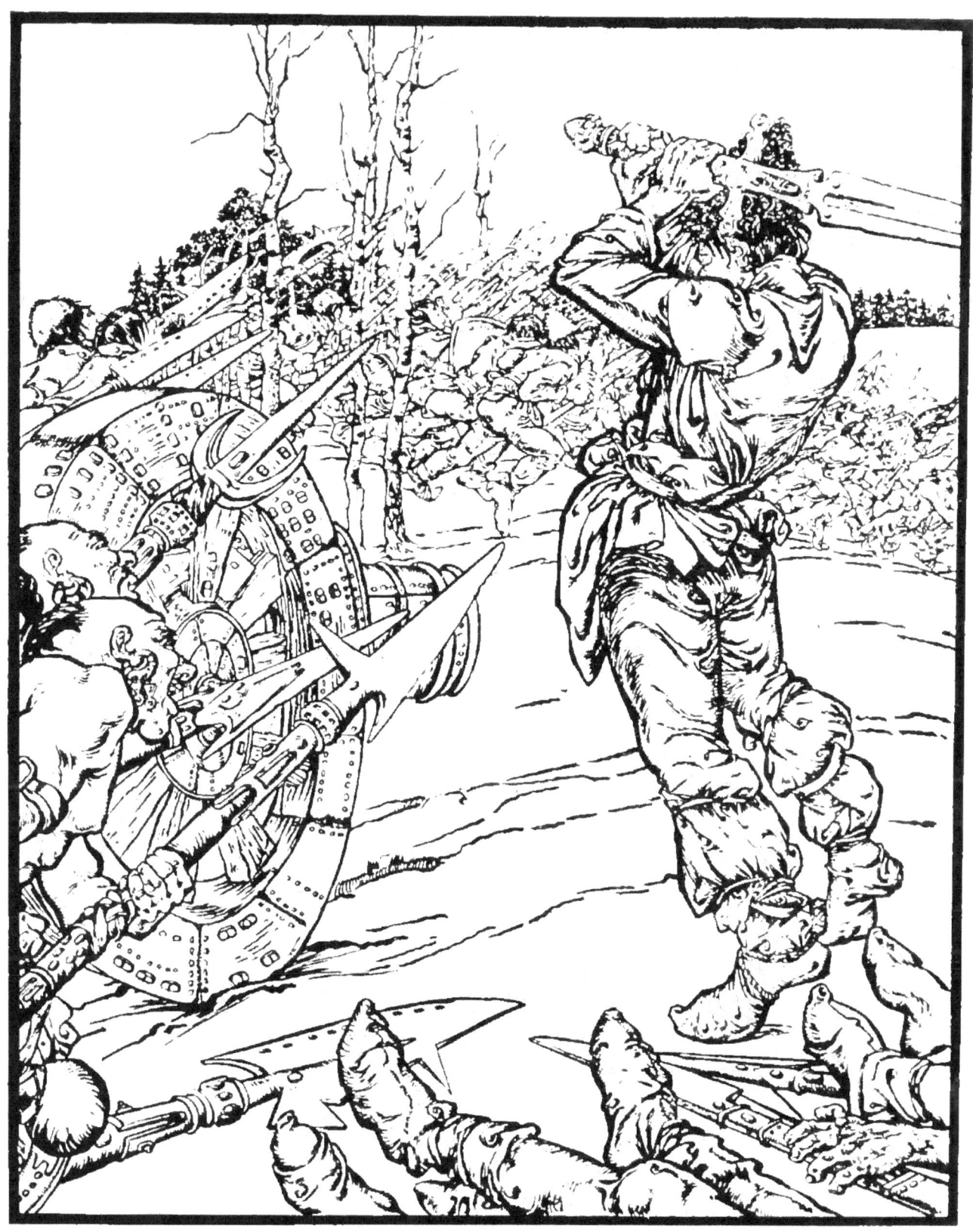

DANIEL WAVED HIS SWORD

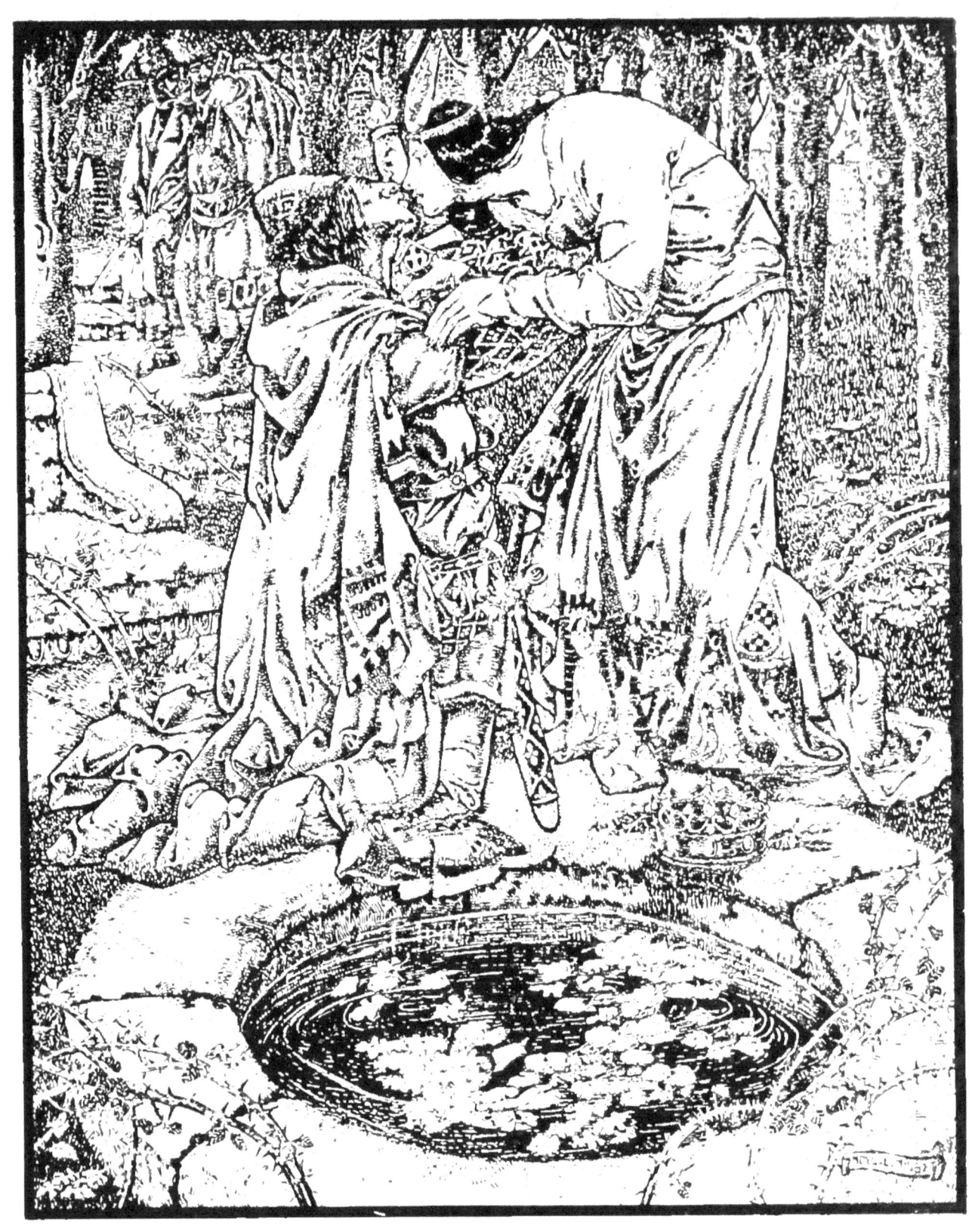

HIS WIFE CARESSED AND WHEEDLED HIM

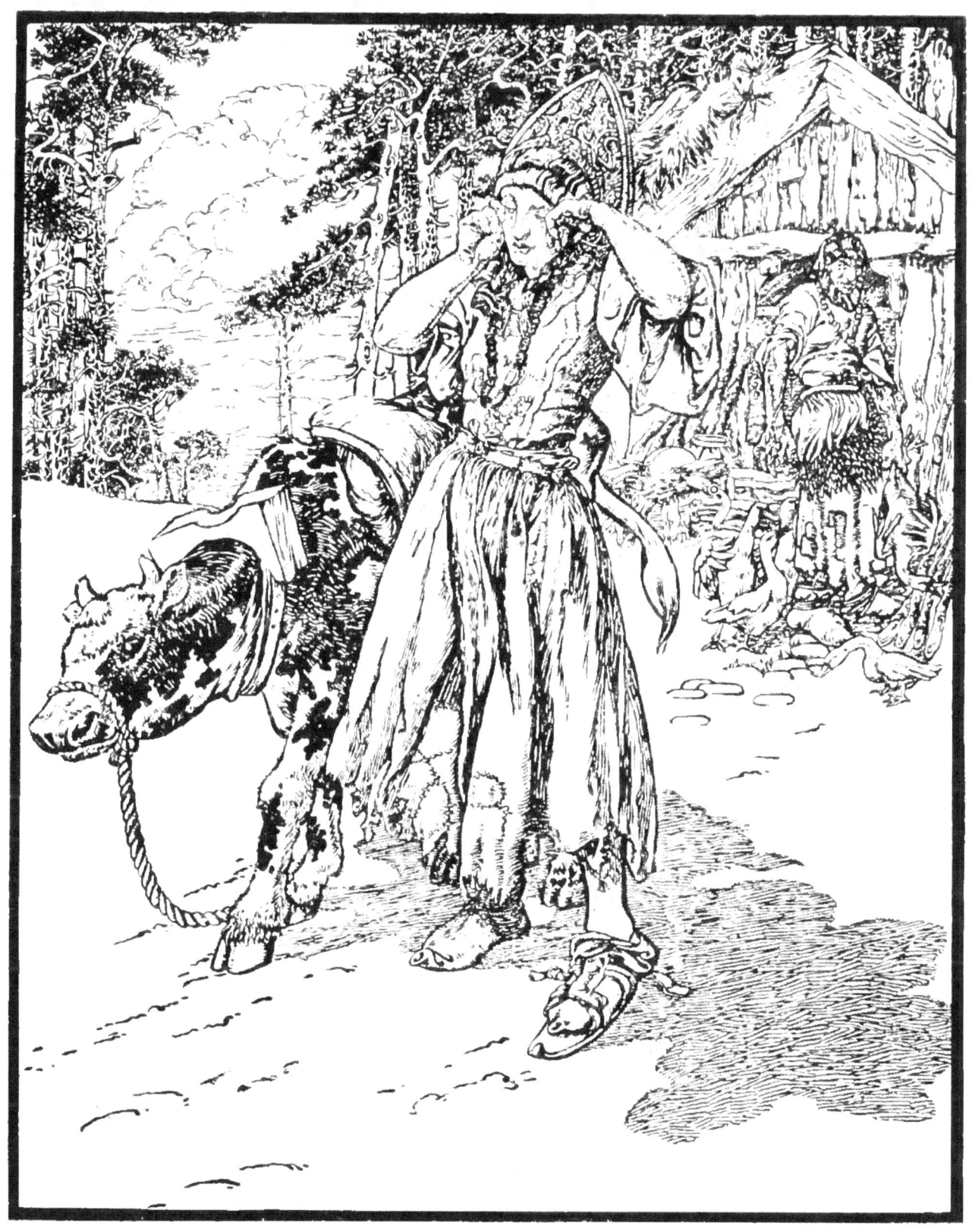

THE GIRL DROVE THE HEIFER OUT TO GRAZE

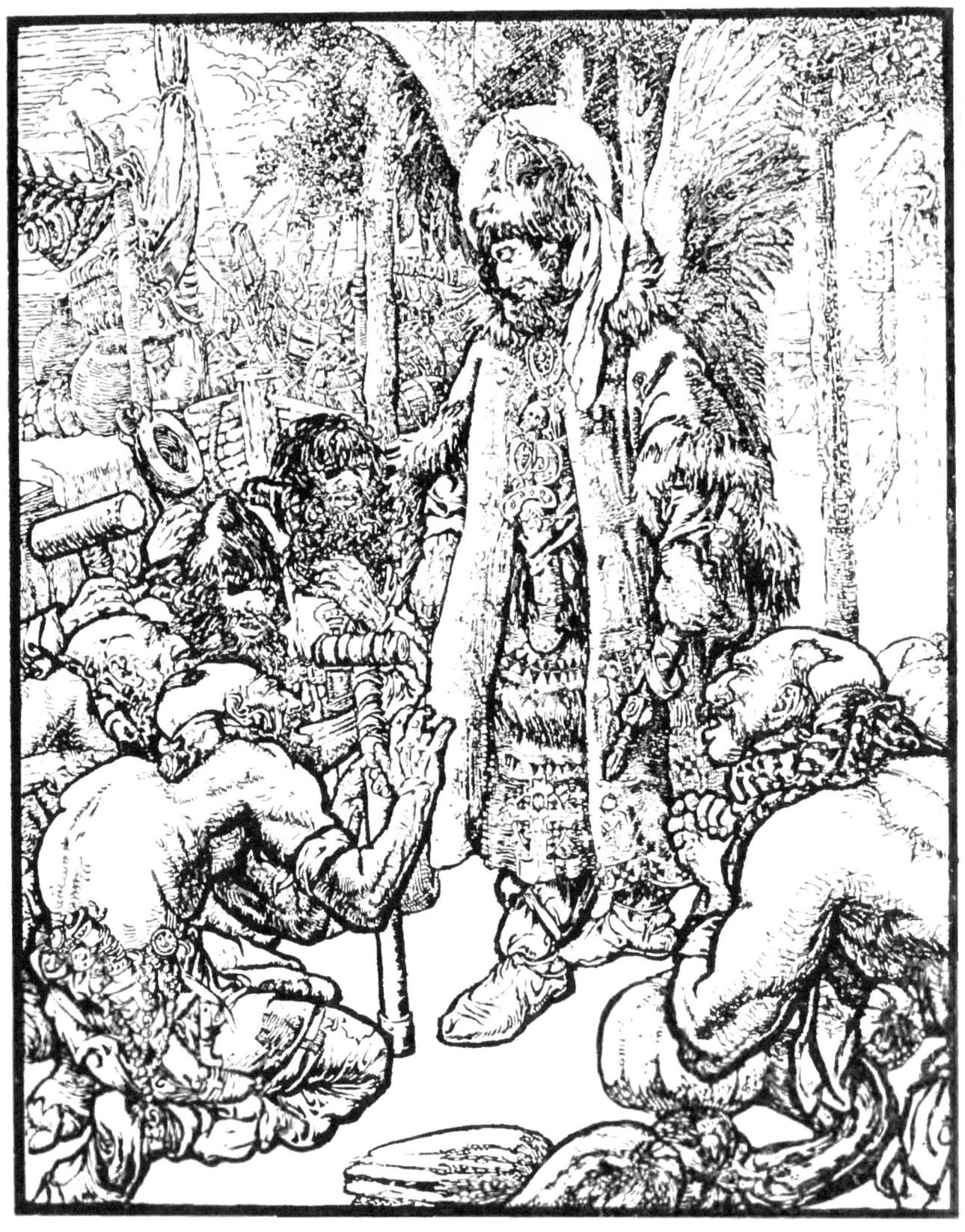

THE TSAR WENT ABOUT INQUIRING OF HIS PEOPLE IF ANY
WERE WRONGED

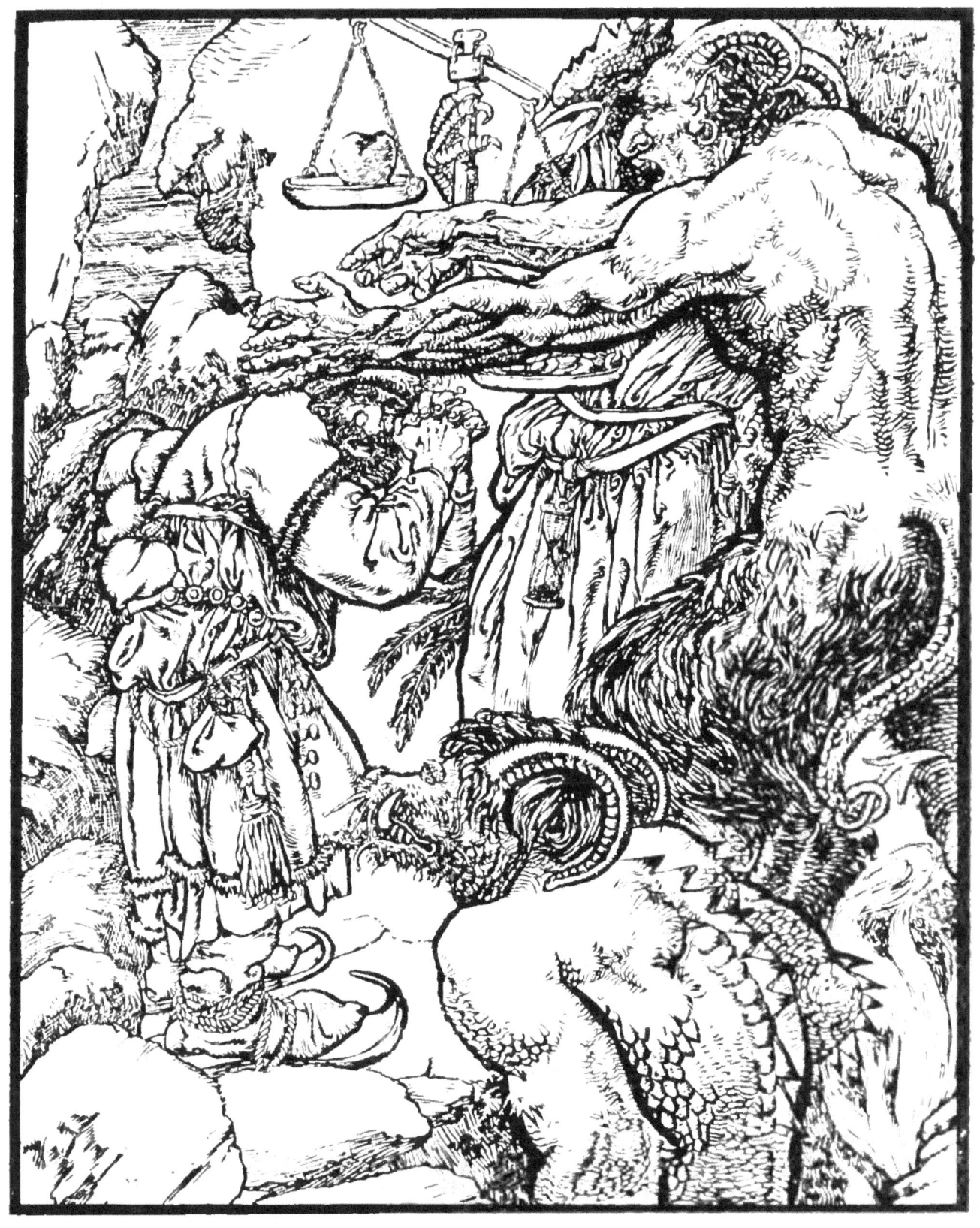

THE RULERS OF HELL LAID HANDS UPON THE OVERSEER
STRAIGHTWAY

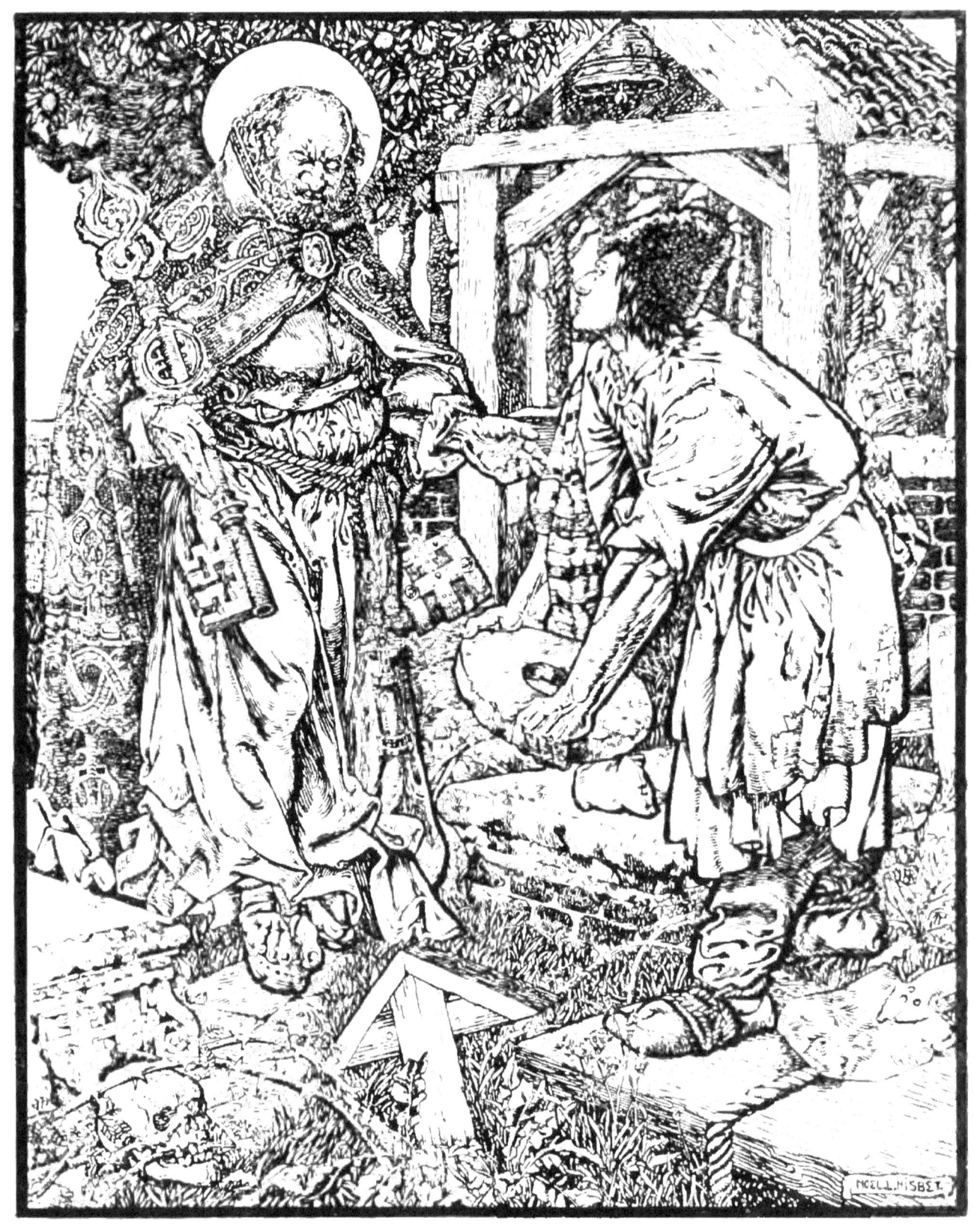

SUDDENLY ST PETER APPEARED TO HIM

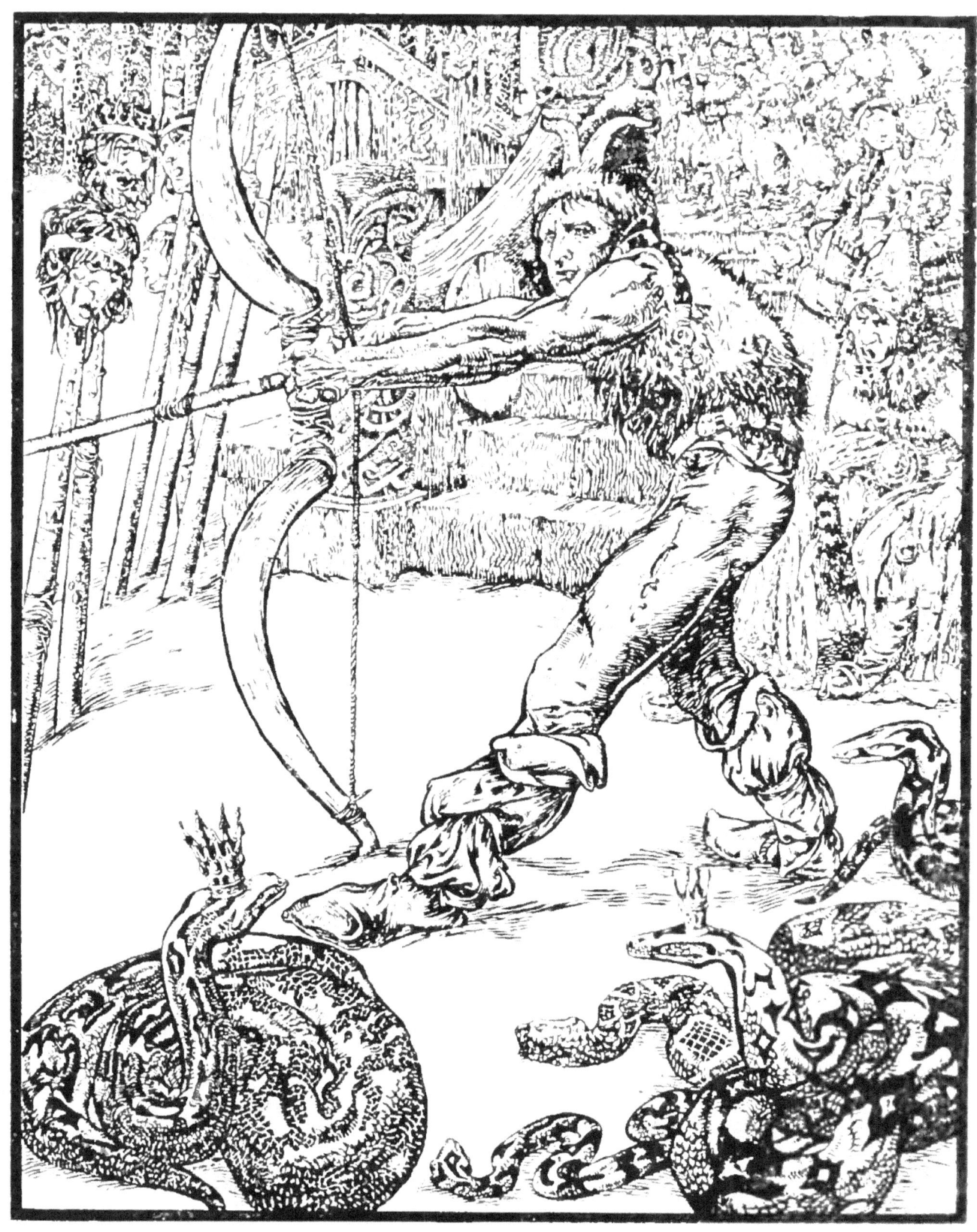

IVAN GOLIK DREW THE BOW

www.ingramcontent.com/pod-product-compliance
Lightning Source LLC
Chambersburg PA
CBHW081619220526
45468CB00010B/2948